THE PROLOGUE
IN THE BEGINNING ...

JOHN SAINSBURY

For Sue, the one who truly completes me and gives me such joy for the journey. Thank you!

THE
PROLOGUE
REFLECTIONS ON GENESIS 1 - 3

The fruit of a seven-year
odyssey, three times over,
at The Limes, Outreach
House and Cocker's
Dyke House: Genesis to
Revelation.

CONTENTS

INTRODUCTION

When you open any book, before the actual story begins, there is often some form of 'prologue' to introduce you to what will follow. Many people might want to skip over these introductory remarks and dive straight into the story, but to do so is sometimes to miss the whole essence of what follows.

In many ways, Genesis 1 to 3 are the chapters that introduce the whole story of the Bible which is to follow. These three chapters are actually part of a larger prologue that extends to the end of Genesis 11. But, for now, we're just going to focus on these three key chapters because it is these, which set the scene and draw the reader into the greatest story ever told.

These chapters have become vitally important for my own understanding of the story I find *myself* in. The complexity of the world we live in, even the make-up of my own body, helped me realise that there had to be more to life than I was experiencing. What these chapters have done is to help me understand not only where life began but why things are the way they are. Ultimately, they gave me hope that there is *way* more to life than meets the eye and that there is an amazing purpose in it all. Without this story, life can easily become an adventure in missing the point. But once the essence of this prologue is seen for what it is then life is truly worth the living.

Sadly, for many people, Christians alike, these chapters have been the source of division and disunity. This is a total tragedy, especially given that this is the beginning of the story that we *all* find ourselves in. This is the story of our world and the story which best describes who we are, where we come from and, ultimately, where we are going.

I hope, in the course of what follows, that you too will find a greater sense of excitement to read the rest of the story and unpack the mysteries of life, death, and life *beyond* death for yourself.

1.
GENESIS 1
In the beginning

In the beginning ...   Genesis 1:1

So begins the greatest story ever told and the beginning of what
I've called the prologue to it. Actually though, this isn't the
beginning at all! This is because, before *our* story really begins
there is *another* story. It is in the fourth word of most of our
English versions that we see this. In this fourth word we meet
the One who was there at the beginning, who was the source of
the beginning, and will ultimately prove to be the one on whom
the whole story rests.

I say it's the fourth word in our *English* Bible because it wasn't
originally written in English: strange though that may sound.

We should be aware, and will become increasingly so, that this creates a slight issue as we go: what we are reading in our English versions is already a translation and thereby an interpretation of the original. Sometimes we'll need to notice and comment on that. But it's what we have and so we continue with it.

In the beginning *God*...   Genesis 1:1

Now, the Bible story doesn't tell us everything we might want to know. It tells us, rather, everything the writers (at least 35 of them based in different times and in different places/cultures) and, ultimately, the One who inspired and directed them think we need to know.

So, if you are reading this and wanting answers to the usual questions that I hear such as: where did Adam and Eve's sons find their wives? Or what happened to the dinosaurs? And so many more, then I'm afraid you might be a little disappointed. Sadly, I can only tell you what the story does say and not what it doesn't. But, be assured, what it *does* say is absolutely *brilliant*. And what it says is that before *our* story began there was a Being that we are introduced to as "God".

Ok, at this point there may be some who are now tempted to stop reading any further: "I don't believe in God" you may say. Here, four words into the story, the reader is faced with their first question: what do I believe about the beginnings of all things? How did all that I know begin? Where did it come from? Where is it going? Why am I here? Do I have any ultimate purpose?

Did something or, better, *Someone* make all this? Or is it just a huge cosmic accident?

The wonderful thing about *this* story is that whilst you are reading it, it is reading *you*! The Bible is like no other book ever written, read or revered. Because this story is alive. And that means that when we have only read the first four words of the prologue, we are already in a position of being asked to consider what we believe. Is there a 'God', an ultimate being?

There are, of course, alternatives: are there many gods or just one? Or is there no higher being at all? Are human beings, the most sophisticated beings we can see operating in our created world, their own masters, their own design and creators? If so; how? Have you ever stopped to wonder what it is that you do believe as opposed to what it is that maybe you don't?

The story makes an incredible claim right at the outset:

In the beginning God *created* ...   Genesis 1:1

Whatever answers you may come up with to the questions above, this is where the story of the Bible begins. The Bible suggests that before the beginning, there was... God. He had to be there to cause the beginning. He 'was', even *before* the beginning! So, this means that what we are reading is the account/story/ description of something that happened directed, so it seems, by the one who did the 'beginning'.

Now of course, this isn't prove-able, one way or another. Whichever way you decide to take this is going to take a matter of 'faith': faith to believe there is 'no God' is still faith in something unproveable, just as much as it is to have 'faith' that there is a God who began it all. But I guess the question is regarding a decision about what makes more sense: that the created order just came out of nowhere or that there was a being ('God') who began it?

> What do you think? And whatever that is, why do you think that? Is what you believe reasonable? What is the evidence to support your theory?

Let us continue: we're only five words in after all!

GOD CREATED EVERYTHING

In the beginning God created *the heavens and the earth.*   Genesis 1:1

So, having made the claim that God existed before the beginning, we now have our second massive challenge to our belief systems. The story states that God created the heavens and the earth. In other words, God, it is claimed here, made *everything*! The skies above, all those stars, moons, planets, etc, etc, all made by God! And the earth, this incredible planet we call our home, with its seas and oceans, deserts and forests, mountains, valleys, etc etc., He, God, created it! All this in one verse!! The story says there's a God who existed before the beginning, and who made EVERYTHING! That's quite a big start, and we're only one verse in! BOOM!!

You could say that verse 1 of Genesis 1 is like the overarching statement that introduces what is to follow. To paraphrase it, v1 says: '**In the beginning God created everything**'. What follows takes that position and unpacks it.

Our 21st Century minds can immediately jump to the functional questions that such a statement raises. Questions like: How did he create it? When did he create it? However, in what follows, whilst we may appear to receive clues to answering those questions, the question that seems to be more at issue is rather: *Why* did he make it?

Genesis 1 leaves us to map out the how and when questions; but that's not God's primary issue. If he's God I guess he could make it in a second, 7 days, or 7 billion years. That really isn't as important as we might imagine. It's the 'why' question that's the one that really matters.

Our writer is keen that we understand the *reason* why God created. And he sets about answering *that* question in the most beautifully artistic way he could. He uses all the writing tricks in the book to make his point. There are complex patterns of word play (all lost on us who don't read it in its original language), poetry, even the number of times certain words are used and how long the sentence structures are. It's very clever stuff! As Rob Bell says in his brilliant unpacking of Genesis 1: "It's almost as if the writer had help".[1]

So, as we progress through what follows in this amazing first

---

1   https://www.youtube.com/watch?v=i2rklwkm_dQ&t=5s

chapter, keep in mind that the writer isn't so keen to answer our questions as he is to ask questions of his own. Questions like: Why does he write it like this? Why provide the information in this way? What's the point of what the writer is saying? My advice in reading these verses is to worry less about interrogating the text and rather let the text interrogate the reader!

Two quick comments: it isn't sexist to refer to the author as 'he': simply the likelihood that the author of such an ancient text would have been male is almost a 'given'.

Also, I want to say that at this point we have recorded the entirety of the first verse of the Bible but it should be noted that when these words were originally recorded there were no chapter and verses included. Someone added them later as a useful way to help people find their way around the text. Did that addition affect the meaning of the text and its understanding? Well, I'd have to say that sometimes it might have! Sometimes, sentence or chapter breaks were added in places that might impact our understanding of what we see before us, and we need to be careful. The Bible might well be the inspired word of God, but we need to be very aware that how we read and understand the version we have of it is not a precise science. That may be a shock to hear but I'd say it is simply a reality to be faced. God (ok, I know He may still up for debate at this point in your thinking) is prepared for some things to be left to us to discern but that's a whole other matter.

But let's get back to Genesis shall we?

GOD CREATED THE EARTH

> Now the earth was formless and empty, darkness was over the surface of the deep, and the Spirit of God was hovering over the waters.
>
> Genesis 1:2

So, having told us in v1 that God made everything, in v2 our attention is immediately focused in on one tiny aspect of God's vast creation: earth.

This is interesting for a start, don't you think!? I'm no physicist but modern cosmology estimates that the universe is some 13.7 billion years old. There are more than 100 billion galaxies in the universe and the average galaxy contains 100 billion stars. Yet the author of Genesis 1 wants to draw our attention to this one single planet among all the rest: earth! Why? Whatever the reason, this is where our author wants us to concentrate our attention. That's not to say that we shouldn't be extremely interested in what else is out there. The universe is incredible. But it's not what our writer is interested in. Straight away our attention is focused on the earth, this "perfect planet" as David Attenborough described it in a BBC documentary of that name.

Now at this stage we are not told anything about how the earth came into being. The writer simply starts the account with the reality that the earth exists.

As we begin our story, we are already made aware that behind it is a God who already existed. And having made everything that exists, it seems, this God is especially concerned with what happens on this tiny (by cosmological concerns) planet we know as earth.

But, at this point, earth doesn't appear to have much going for it. Our writer describes it as "formless and empty," and with "darkness over the surface of the deep". The picture this conjures up in my mind is that of a lump of clay on a potter's wheel. There's potential there but until the potter gets going all you have is the potentiality. The earth here seems to be like any other planet we see through the wonders of modern telescopes; the words formless and empty really say it all. Darkness evokes negative thoughts too. 'Light' is a much more positive thought and this suggests everything that is its opposite: but we'll return to that in a moment. Here the stage seems set for something to happen, but what? And who's going to make a difference to this setting? Verse 2 not only tells us the situation but points forward to who is going to step in to make the difference: "and the Spirit/ Wind of God was hovering over the waters."

Now here is where biblical interpretation gets interesting. You remember me mentioning that the bible wasn't originally written in English? Well, this section was originally written in Hebrew and the word here translated "Spirit", could equally be translated 'Wind' or 'Breath'. It is really the connected word "hovering" that leads interpreters to consider the word "Spirit" as offering the best translation for our English Bibles.

Again, that word 'hovering' is evocative. Think for a moment of a creature that might hover. In my mind's eye I see a hawk, seemingly stationery in the sky looking down above its prey yet only able to stay in that place because its wings are beating very fast. There it hangs waiting for the moment, the right moment to dive into action. In verse 2 it seems there is something/someone "hovering over the waters". Our writer isn't concerned with how the waters got there or when, that is simply assumed as part of the creation that we read of in verse 1. But over this formless and empty planet, with darkness over the surface of the deep, there hovers the Spirit of God just waiting to move, waiting for the action to commence.

THE SPIRIT OF GOD

Before we jump to that though, here we are being introduced to an aspect of God that we need to get our heads round. This God we met in v1, has a "Spirit."

So, before we go any further, what would you say is meant by that word "spirit"? What is a "spirit"?

A quick look in my dictionary suggests a "spirit" is traditionally believed to be 'the vital principle or animating force within living beings'. So, we could see this Spirit or Wind as the animating force of God acting within creation. He/she/it seems to be God at work, or at least about to be, within this creation. And his/her/its activities are focused on this earth. God is about to do something and as we move onto verse 3, we'll find out what that entails.

And God said, "Let there be light," and there was light.   Genesis 1:3

19

Again, this short sentence is crammed to overflowing with incredible delights and implications and there is so much to say I almost don't know where to begin! But begin we must and, for starters, this verse sets the scene for the creation narrative that is to follow. It is a beautifully structured initiation of the standard formulae that our writer uses to unpack each stage of the creation. And this formula has seven parts to it.

Something that occurs throughout the Bible is the importance of numbers as well as words. The number seven, for reasons that will become apparent later, is often used to symbolise perfection. The point here seems to be that this creation that is about to be described is, at least to begin with, perfect.

Wenham describes these seven stages as: [2]

1) announcement, "God said"
2) command, "let there be"
3) fulfilment, "it was so"
4) execution, "light'
5) approval, "saw... good"
6) subsequent word, "God called"
7) day number.

So, the verse begins with an announcement: "And God said". Now my first, and perhaps the most obvious question is, how do we know God said this? Only God was there?! Whoever wrote the creation account seemingly had access to the only source

2   G.J. Wenham, *Genesis 1-15: Word Biblical Commentary*, Waco, Texas: Word, 1987, p17

that could know this information. As we progress through this chapter, we'll come across that phrase a further nine times (vv 6, 9, 11, 14, 20, 24, 26, 28, 29), making ten in all: another important symbolic number in biblical thought.

But back to this first announcement: God says it and, we discover increasingly as we read on, what He says goes! God only has to say it and it's as good as done. Whatever else that tells us, the point here seems to be that this God has absolute authority.

LET THERE BE LIGHT

So, what is it that God announces? "Light"

Those who are scientifically minded might balk at this perhaps. The thing is, it's not until day 4 of creation that we read of the creation of our light source, the sun. So, whatever this light is, it isn't that. So, what is meant by this 'light'?

> Before we go any further, just pause for a moment and ask yourself that question: what do you think is meant by 'light' here?

I saw an interesting thing recently; scientists have discovered that at the moment of fertilisation a small burst of light is emitted.[3] This made me think that maybe, in some sense, this verse is describing the ultimate moment of new creation: a new life is

3   https://www.sciencealert.com/scientists-just-captured-the-actual-flash-of-light-that-sparks-when-sperm-meets-an-egg

being made as the work of creation begins. It's like planet earth is about to come to life!

Others observe that in the Bible 'light' is often used as a contrast to 'darkness'. Indeed, in v2 we read that "darkness was over the surface of the deep". In contrast to that darkness, which was described as connected to an earth that was "formless and empty" v2, now God commands 'light'. No longer will this earth be formless, empty and dark. What God is bringing into being is a planet that is the direct opposite of that: a planet full of form and life and vibrancy. The earth is being brought to life at God's command. And we don't need to wait too long to see God's verdict on this:

> God saw that the light was good, and he separated the light from the darkness.
> Genesis 1:4

It's interesting that God doesn't say the "darkness" was bad! But we can see that, as he looks at the "light", it is certainly the light that receives God's favour. God separates the light from the darkness. 'Separation' is a concept/instruction that recurs frequently in the early verses of Genesis 1, notably in days 1-3. From day 4 to 6 this separation is superseded by God's 'filling'. More of that later. Separation is also a theme we meet throughout the biblical story and one which finds its ultimate culmination in the separation of humanity into two distinct groupings: those who have faith in Jesus and those who don't. In fact, maybe there's another separation being hinted at here!

Now, some of you might be saying here; just a minute why

are you suddenly talking about Jesus? Well let's just take a quick excursion and jump forward in the biblical story to the beginnings of what we know as the New Testament (we'll leave explanations of words like Testament for another time; but suffice to say that the Bible is a book 'separated' into two sections we know as the Old and New Testaments). If we turn to the New Testament for a moment and open our Bibles at the beginning of the book we know as John (we call the first four books of the New Testaments "Gospels" meaning "good news" because these are stories of the best news the world ever had), we find something very interesting.

This is how the Gospel of John begins: "In the beginning...."
John 1:1

> Now if we pause there for a second, does anything sound familiar here? We've heard that phrase before! The Gospel writer seems to be drawing a deliberate parallel to how the Old Testament story began. So, let's read on:

"In the beginning was the Word, and the Word was with God, and the Word was God."
John 1:1

IN THE BEGINNING WAS THE WORD

Now things could get very complicated at this point; but I want to keep this as simple as possible. When we looked at how the Old Testament story began right back at the beginning, we encountered God, who's Spirit was hovering over the surface of the deep waiting for the get-go. And then in Genesis 1:3 we heard the voice of God speak saying: "Let there be light." As we open John's story of the life, death and resurrection of Jesus, his gospel, we begin with 'the Word' (the voice, the one who spoke) and we read that the Word was with God, and the Word was God John 1:1.

This seems reasonable enough; the one who spoke creation into being has a voice: he speaks "words" and, as we saw, when he speaks them things happen. So far so good. But when John begins his story of Jesus, he begins by speaking of this voice/ Word as if it is somehow separate to God yet at the same time one with God. It's a bit like how we read that the Spirit of God was hovering over the waters. This is the Spirit *of God*. So the Spirit is God's Spirit connected completely to him, yet strangely described as if separate from him.

If your mind is beginning to explode right now, don't worry it's about to get worse! Listen to what John goes on to say:

In the beginning was the Word, and the Word was with God, and the Word was God. He was with God in the beginning. Through him all things were made; without him nothing was made that has been made.

Remember us saying earlier that another way of reading Genesis 1:1 was simply: "In the beginning God made everything". Well now this *making* is being ascribed to the Word of God as if that 'Word' were somehow separate from God whilst still being one with him.

In him was life; and that life was the light of all mankind. The light shines in the darkness, and the darkness has not overcome it.

Just as in the Genesis account, John begins his account by describing how light came into the darkness – interesting!

There was a man sent from God whose name was John. (By whom he meant John the Baptist not the John who wrote this gospel. – ed.) He came as a witness to testify concerning that light, so that through him all might believe. He himself was not the light; he came only a witness to the light. The true light that gives light to everyone was coming into the world. He was in the world, and though the world was made through him, the world did not recognize him. He came to that which was his own, but his own did not receive him. Yet to all who did receive him, to those who believed in his name, he gave the right to become children of God – children born not of natural descent, nor of human decision or a husband's will, but born of God.

And here's possibly the most remarkable statement ever recorded:

The Word became flesh and made his dwelling among us. We have seen his glory, the glory of the one and only Son, who came from the Father, full of grace and truth.   John 1:1-14

THE WORD BECAME FLESH

In this most amazing, mind-blowing introduction to his account of the life, death and resurrection of Jesus, the apostle John is *deliberately* saying that the Jesus that he spent 3 years being apprenticed to, the man he knew, followed around, listened to, ate with, watched intently for 3 years turns out to be none other than... the same *God* who made the world. Yet what he says is not quite as blunt as that. It's like he's trying to describe Jesus as being one with God, yet somehow simultaneously suggesting that he's somehow, dare I say it, separate from him.

If it was a crazy enough claim to suggest that behind this amazing creation is a creator God who spoke it all into being, then the craziness just went to a whole other level. *The Creator's Word, according to John, became like one of the created.* He became a human being. If we're talking about separation, then this has to be the most epic separation imaginable: Jesus, who we know as the Son, was somehow separated from the fulness he had at the beginning with his Father (God). The light of the world, who spoke creation into being at the very outset of the story, took on flesh and blood.[4] What a story!

Maybe at this stage we should pause afresh and give ourselves a few moments to consider the most outrageous claim ever made: outrageous, that is, unless it's true.

> Again, the text raises the question of us: Who do people say Jesus was? What are the implications of that claim? Who do *you* say Jesus was/is? There is probably no bigger issue that each and every one of us needs to get our heads round.

So, let us pause now and summarise where we are up to. In just the first few verses of the Bible story, at the beginning of our

4   I love how the apostle Paul describes this in Philippians 2:5-8

prologue, we've learned that *before* the beginning of creation there already existed a Being known as 'God'. This Being, as well as being the one before the beginning, is certainly 'one' but is described in ways that seem to make him more than one, a community if you like, yet completely one at the same time.[5]

This God has a Spirit who seems to be involved actively in creation. He also has a voice, who later in the story took on humanity's flesh and blood and entered the very creation He had spoken into life. This "Son", as we shall later get to know him, was known as Jesus and the New Testament writers have plenty to say about him. But we're not up to that in the story just now. We began with the voice of God bringing forth "light", and there was light, and God declared it "good" v4. Thereafter we begin a series of separations as God gets to work on "project earth" setting the scene for the story that is to follow.

So, let's get back to the story as we pick it up in v5:

WE REST THEN WE WORK

God called the light "day," and the darkness he called "night." And there was evening and there was morning – the first day. Genesis 1:5

Now, as we mentioned, this is a pattern/formulae we will see repeated constantly through this first chapter (remembering of

5   Bilezikian describes the Trinity as a 'community of oneness' in:
    G. Bilezikian, *Community 101*, Grand Rapids, Michigan: Zondervan, p18

course that the boundaries of what constitutes the "chapter" were set later). But there are some strange anomalies we need to note before we go on!

For a start the way we (well, certainly the culture I'm a part of) count a day, is from day to night. But in this text, a day is being counted as moving from evening to morning. In other words, from darkness to light; from night to day. In our thinking, we work then we rest. But the idea in this biblical way of marking time is that we rest and then we work. This has so much to tell us about the whole way we have come to view the world and how different it is to biblical thought.

For us, we work first, then we rest. But the pattern of biblical thought is much more gracious. What this verse is showing subtly us is that God's pattern works the other way around. We rest first, then we work. We might even say that grace (we rest) comes before we've done anything (our works).[6] We rest in God and let him keep us alive and breathing and it's only out of that rest that we 'do' anything ourselves. In the pattern of biblical thought, darkness comes first and then there is light.

Furthermore, looking again at the way John began his Gospel account, he describes the 'Word made flesh' as the one who was the light of the world who came to a world that was effectively in the dark in order to bring his light. Darkness is destroyed by the emergence of light; darkness cannot snuff out the light; but, rather, the light destroys the darkness (John 1:5).

6   The idea that we are saved by grace through faith and not by our works is picked up by the apostle Paul who wrote a good deal of the rest of the New Testament see for example Ephesians 2:8-9

But there's more here. Before the creation of the sun, which enables us to mark time into day and night, the work of creating light is the sole task God performed on this first day. What we are about to read is that the work of creation is set out over a 7-day cycle. From this we arrive at the pattern of our own week. God creates for six days and then finally, when creation is complete, he rests. This is the pattern that human beings are to emulate. Life isn't all about work. But neither is it just about rest. We need both. And when God sets about his work of creation he does so in a beautifully structured way.

We might think of it a bit like building the stage for a play being put on in a theatre; there is a carefully structured process of setting the scene. But all that is only to support the main event when the actors arrive on stage to perform the actual play. What we have, as these 'days' of creation unwind, is the backdrop to the principal actors arriving; but that won't be for another five days. What the writer does, in a beautifully crafted, poetic framework, is show us that creation was God's planned, structured and purposeful work to create something out of nothing, light out of darkness, life out of death. The first day has been completed and when God saw the "light", he declared it "good" v4. I love that! God stands back from the work he's done and says in effect: "I'm pleased with that"!

Okay, time for another 'pause for thought' moment. Some questions for us to reflect on: How does the structure of these verses speak into the balance of our lives? Have we got the balance right of rest and work: we need both! How well do we plan the activities of our lives,

> are we haphazard or is there a good structure that we follow? Do we, do you, allow ourselves moments of standing back and reviewing the work we've done and commending ourselves on what we have achieved? Do you allow yourself the enjoyment and fulfilment of "and it was good" moments?

Day one is now over: it's time to progress to our second day of creation.

WATERS ABOVE AND BELOW

And God said, "Let there be a vault between the waters to separate water from water.

Genesis 1:6

Now I don't know about you, but controlling water isn't really one of my specialities. Water goes where it goes. But here we read, that on the second day, God does some pretty cool controlling over the waters. If we read on the next verses explain:

So God made the vault and separated the water under the vault from the water above it. And it was so. God called the vault "sky." And there was evening, and there was morning – the second day.

Genesis 1:7-8

Confession time: I'm a bit of 'news-aholic'. I like to watch the daily news and then catch the weather forecast at the tail-end. Over the years forecasters have become much more adept at forecasting what is likely to happen in the coming day(s). Essentially, where I live it isn't too hard to predict: it'll tend to be some variety of cool and wet, wet and cool. But, if you stop to think about it, our whole weather system is incredible. Water evaporates from the oceans and seas, winds blow weather systems containing that water vapour around the globe and then fresh water falls on the earth as rain. Meanwhile, the sun keeps our temperature just right for life to exist. And occasionally things in the skies get cold enough for the waters from above to be deposited either as snow or hail. Weather is amazing and the total extent of my interaction with it is generally to complain that too much of the rain is falling in my neck of the woods and we're receiving too little sun!

Essentially, on day 2, God is setting up the weather system and providing the canvas for two zones of life to exist. We'll get to the filling of these zones on day 5. Now I don't know what our human ancestors would have understood by the space between earth and sky, here described as a "vault", but our writer is making it clear that this Creator God has total control even over the waters: even the seas, even the weather! And here I can't resist jumping forward a bit again to a well-known story about Jesus found in Mark's gospel. Mark 4:35-41. It's so good, let me tell it to you:

That day when evening came, he said to his disciples, "Let us go over to the other side." Leaving the crowds behind, they took him along, just as he was, in the boat. There were also other boats with him. A furious squall came up, and the waves broke over the boat, so that it was nearly swamped. Jesus was in the stern, sleeping on a cushion. The disciples woke him and said to him, "Teacher, don't you care if we drown?" He got up, rebuked the wind and said to the waves, "Quiet! Be still!" Then the wind died down and it was completely calm. He said to his disciples, "Why are you so afraid? Do you still have no faith?" They were terrified and asked each other, "Who is this? Even the wind and the waves obey him!"

Mark 4:35-41

Do you notice anything about this strange and amazing story? Jesus, there's that man again, is in a boat with his disciples, many hardy fishermen who you'd expect to be used to storms at sea, but apparently not this one! So, this storm at sea was a biggy and the disciples are terrified they are going to drown. Don't you just love it that Jesus is so not bothered that he's fast asleep! But when they wake him, and he sees their terror he does something quite remarkable: He got up, rebuked the wind and said to the waves, "Quiet! Be still!"

Jesus it seems, only has to say the words and the waters above (the weather) and the waters below (the seas) do what *he* says! It's another 'And it was so' moment. Now, I've heard people describe Jesus as a good man, a good teacher but nothing more. To them I want to ask: how many good teachers, and good men can control the waters above and the waters below like this? No wonder the disciples asked: "Who is this? Even the wind and the waves obey him!"

If day 2 was the second day of separation and forming, when we come to day 3, we arrive at the third:

And God said, "Let the water under the sky be gathered to one place, and let dry ground appear." And it was so. God called the dry ground "land," and the gathered waters he called "seas." And God saw that it was good. Genesis 1:9-10

LAND AND SEA

Genesis isn't the only place in the Bible where God's creative works are described. If you flick forward to the Psalms, which are a collection of majestic poems/songs found roughly in the middle of our Bibles, we find examples of songs/poems of praise to God for his works of creative genius. Have a look at Psalm 104 for example: it puts the words of these verses into a more expanded tribute to God's handiwork. It culminates in the only real response to what God has done: Praise the LORD, my soul. Praise the LORD. Psalm 104:35b.

Day 2 was the vertical aspect of separation: the waters above were separated from the waters below. On day 3 we have the horizontal separation of waters whereby dry ground is separated into land and seas. Both axes are necessary to complete the backdrop to the story; vertical *and* horizontal. This reminds me again of that man Jesus.

Having displayed his prowess over nature, over sickness and even over death (you'll need to read the gospels to read about all this), you might have thought that Jesus would be given a fair amount of reverence and respect. Sadly, as we read on in the story, whilst some seem to recognize the incredible nature of this man, others see him as a dangerous upstart who needs to be removed as soon as possible. The religious leaders in Israel manipulate the ruling overseers of Rome in order to have Jesus nailed to a Roman cross where he died in the most excruciatingly painful way humans had hitherto devised. There, he too experienced the two axes of a vertical and a horizontal cross

beam as he was nailed to each! In that awful separation of
Jesus, he completed the ultimate work of reconciliation: the
most significant that the world has ever known. Jesus is the one
whose death on the cross reconnects the realms of the heavens
above to the earth below (the vertical axis). In other words
Jesus reconnects us to God. He also reaches out to all peoples
with his (horizontal) open arms of love. We'll touch more on
that story later. For now, let us focus on the fulness of God's
creative action on day 3.

So, now we have three separations: darkness and light; waters
above and waters below; and now dry ground called 'land' and
waters called 'seas'. We should note that it is God who calls the
dry ground "land" and the waters "seas", just as earlier it was
God who called the light "day" and the darkness "night" v5. In
the ancient Near East, if a King named a thing or even a person,
this was an act of claiming dominion over it.

This is the dynamic that we see a bit later in Genesis 17:5. There,
God called one man, Abram (meaning something like 'exalted
father'), and changed his name to Abraham (probably meaning
'father of many'); in doing so, he's giving an indication of the
plans that God had for him. By giving Abram a new name, God
was effectively calling Abram to serve him.

But, before we get too distracted by Abraham, and I could easily
do so, we need to go back to Genesis 1. Here, we should note
that because God is naming the great cosmic realities of day and
night, sky, land and seas, our writer is reminding us that these
things are under God's oversight not ours. Bear this in mind

when we move on in the chapter and note who gets to do the naming of other aspects of creation!

With land and seas separated out in v11 we discover that God had big plans for the land he'd just separated out:

> Then God said, "Let the land produce vegetation: seed-bearing plants and trees on the land that bear fruit with seed in it, according to their various kinds. And it was so. The land produced vegetation: plants bearing seed according to their kinds and trees bearing fruit with seed in it according to their kinds. And God saw that it was good. And there was evening and there was morning – the third day.
>
> Genesis 1:11-13

VEGETATION

I love the understatement of it all. God's word being spoken out is like seeds being sown enabling the ground to produce vegetation. (I wonder if Jesus had this idea in mind when he told the parable of the sower in Mark 4:1-20. If you don't know it, then why not flick forward in your Bible and have a quick read!)

So, here again, God speaks, and life appears. This time, however, that life has the capacity to recreate itself! Seed-bearing plants and trees are, in themselves, capable of producing more of the same. God starts the process off and then effectively says: 'away you go'! I've always been fascinated by seeds. Tiny things that when planted in soil, with the right amount of moisture and light, can replicate the initial plant and then ultimately produce more seeds that enable the process to continue. It's shear genius! The capacity that each seed has, from such a tiny start, to grow into something matching and even larger than the original plant is phenomenal. One of my favourite examples of this is an acorn. When compared to an oak tree of many years growth I am always blown away by the potentiality each seed contains. It seems Jesus delighted in this process too, using the amazing potential of a mustard seed to explain the potentiality of even a little bit of faith in a person's life (Mark 4:30-32).

Another thing to note here is the sheer quantity and variety of different plants that are found on this planet we call home. I have no idea what the number would be, but God doesn't do things by halves. Just take a walk around your average garden and count how many different varieties of tree and plant you find (if you can) and allow the enormity of it all to let you marvel! But there is some order to this too! There is that interesting refrain repeated here: "according to their kinds". In fact, three times we read this expression which is surely making an important point for us to grasp. Whilst there is an absolute abundance of variety to the vegetation God produces, it is far from haphazard. There are boundaries, different groupings, "kinds". And again, when God looks at this incredible variety of trees, shrubs, flowers, grasses and the like, we have that other repeated refrain of incredible understatement: And God saw that it was *good*. And there was evening and there was morning – the third day v13.

FILLING UP: HE ALSO MADE THE STARS

As we move into the fourth day, we also move from days of forming to days of filling.

And God said, "Let there be lights in the vault of the sky to separate the day from the night, and let them serve as signs to mark sacred times, and days and years, and let them be lights in the vault of the sky to give light on the earth. And it was so. God made two great lights – the greater light to govern the day and the lesser light to govern the night. He also made the stars. God set them in the vault of the sky to give light on the earth, to govern the day and the night, and to separate light from darkness. And God saw that it was good. And there was evening, and there was morning - the fourth day.

Genesis 1:14-19

In the midst of these verses is one of, if not *the*, greatest understatements ever recorded: He also made the stars. What!? God made the stars? Something of the sheer enormity of the stars really struck me when I saw Louie Giglio's talk: *How Great is Our God.*[7] If you've never watched it, I'd encourage you to do so with a golf ball in hand (you'll see what I mean if you have a look).

The universe is vast, unbelievably vast. To get some idea how vast, how's this for an amazing claim: there are more stars in the sky than there are grains of sand on planet earth. Don't believe me? Well read this in the footnote.[8]

7   https://www.youtube.com/watch?v=atUGBua2AzE
8   https://www.npr.org/sections/krulwich/2012/09/17/161096233/which-is-greater-the-number-of-sand-grains-on-earth-or-stars-in-the-sky?t=1613134090243

Both in terms of the bigness and the smallness of stars and molecules, the created universe blows my mind. And the mention the stars get here is laughable: He (God) also made the stars. I hope this simple line of text starts to make you appreciate the whole nature of the God we're talking about here; and equally the absolute absurdity of the claim that this same Word of God who spoke those stars into being became a flesh and blood human! This is such a crazy story; unless it's true. But if it's true then everything about the way we view the world, and our own lives, has to change. That was certainly the case for me!

I can remember when I first started hearing about this God, hearing the claims about Jesus, and even the 'ridiculous' suggestion that this God was actually interested in me. I could hardly take it in. I used to stand outside on a starry night and speak to the void and say: "God if you are real, would you please move that star across the sky, then I'll know it's true!" I have to tell you that God never succumbed to my challenge. God doesn't do 'light shows' of that nature I'm sad to say. But, now I think about it, the whole vast array of space was surely evidence enough of something – someone way beyond my experience or comprehension. And all this is covered in that simple line: He also made the stars. There are many who want to debate the 'hows' and the 'whens' of this claim. But all the text seems interested in telling us is that God said: "let there be…" "and it was so".

God made our two great lights too: the sun and the moon to govern the day and the night to mark out the day and night. So on 'day' 4 we arrive at the creation of the 'day' makers. For those who want to debate how this could be then I'd recommend a reading of John Lennox's little book *Seven Days That Divide the World*.[9]

There have been many human cultures throughout history that paid special attention to the stars. Even today in many daily newspapers, claims are made that the movement of the stars affects the things that happen to us in our daily lives. Even the Bible seems to agree that certain events on earth can be foretold by the movement of the heavenly bodies.[10]

The two great lights, the sun and the moon, principally govern the day and the night but they also serve as signs to 'mark sacred times, and days and years'. There's so much more to this than I know or understand. But the writer is clear that, in contrast to the thinking of many ancient Near Eastern understandings of the heavenly bodies, the lights we see in the sky are not gods, nor are they capable of controlling our lives. Rather, they are creations of the God of Genesis who simply speaks them into being and commands them to provide light on earth, greater by day and lesser by night, and to determine the earthly calendar. The earth remains the central aspect of God's concern even if science demonstrates that the earth orbits the sun and not vice versa.

I love it that humans are now venturing into space to explore our immediate planetary neighbours. How incredible it is to think that humans have now walked on the surface of the moon. But still the greater claim remains that the one who *made* the moon, the sun and the stars walked upon the earth![11]

9   J.C.Lennox, *Seven Days that divide the World*, Grand Rapids, Michigan: Zondervan, 2011, p39-66
10 Matthew 2:1-2
11 John 1:14

Once more, God seems to stand back and say to himself: 'not a bad day's work, that'. Or as the writer puts it: And God saw that it was good. And there was evening, and there was morning – the fourth day Genesis 1:18b-19. And there we have it: a setting of the sun and the rising of the same to confirm it!

FILLING UP: THE SKIES AND SEAS

So, to the fifth day and the filling out of the waters above (the skies) and the waters below (the seas). Here is the filling up of those aspects of creation that were separated out on day 2.

> And God said, "Let the water teem with living creatures, and let birds fly above the earth across the vault of the sky." So God created the great creatures of the sea and every living thing with which the water teems and that moves about in it, according to their kinds, and every winged bird according to its kind. And God saw that it was good. God blessed them and said, "Be fruitful and increase in number and fill the water in the seas, and let birds increase on earth." And there was evening and there was morning — the fifth day
> Genesis 1:20-23

There is a slight change in our word pattern here as God doesn't 'name' the creatures he makes; those who will fill the waters and skies are to be named by a source other than God. Rather, God "Blessed them" and commanded them to be fruitful and increase in number. To "bless" is one of those rather strange religious-sounding words that probably doesn't mean much to the average person in the street but that has some sort of general connotation of wishing the best for someone, wishing them well or wishing them favour. In other words, as God's creative splendour moves to a whole new level, He desires nothing but the best for these incredible, varied and wonderful creatures that He gives life to.

It's one thing for God to put in place vegetation that will produce the seeds to reproduce, but think for a moment of the sort of mind that makes the creatures of the seas or the beautiful variety of the birds of the air. As at the time of writing it is estimated that there are somewhere in the region of 10,000 different species of bird that we know of (though new research puts that at more like 18,000) and something like 34,000 different species of fish. God doesn't scrimp on creativity even when it comes to the waters, where human beings rarely even see! If you've ever watched a documentary about the natural world you'll be amazed at the variety of shapes and sizes, colours and mating techniques that the birds and the fish, in all their vast array, have been *blessed* to do. That birds can fly, leaving the earth and flying under their own steam is truly magnificent. Just as I recommended holding a seed and considering its potentiality, see if you can find a feather. When you find one just take a look at the utter amazing creation you hold in your hand: what a design!

Again, we see that there are boundaries here to be observed. The birds and fish are to multiply, yes, but there is the boundary of their different kinds: v21. As we've seen there is an order to the way God is fashioning his created world, one that presumably we would do well to observe and maintain. This ordering and non-mixing is something that recurs when the peculiar rules of non mixing are described in the book of Leviticus (one of my personal favourites). Yet, God desires abundance. I love that expression: "Let the water *teem* with living creatures". The creator God that we are encountering here is the least stingy being there is. His approach to creating is basically 'the more the merrier'!

Some of those sea creatures are pretty massive too. We read that God created the *great creatures* of the sea v21. The blue whale is probably the biggest sea creature we know of; some measuring the region of 33 metres long. To put that into perspective, that's about two-thirds the height of Nelson's column in Trafalgar Square. The maximum recorded weight of one of these great creatures is in the region of 190 tonnes. Understandably, many ancient cultures perceived some of these great creatures as enemies to be feared. But, in the Genesis account, these are creatures made by God that He commanded to go forth and make more of themselves and fill the vast oceans that He had made. Again, we are not told how this happened, nor in what time frame. God speaks all these creatures into being with the mandate to make more of themselves and somehow He knows how that should be done. It's tragic to think that through overfishing and through ruining their natural habitats mankind is actually putting many of these species at risk of extinction. But that is to get ahead of ourselves. For now, we have seas teeming with life and birds soaring in the skies and, as He sees all this, once again God says: it's good!

WE REACH THE CLIMAX

And so we come to the sixth day. The account now feels as though we are coming to the climax of the whole creative adventure. There are three aspects to the sixth day and we'll consider each in turn beginning with the creation of the animals that will 'fill' the land.

And God said, "Let the land produce living creatures according to their kinds; the livestock, the creatures that move along the ground, and the wild animals, each according to its kind. And it was so.

God made the wild animals according to their kinds, the livestock according to their kinds, and all the creatures that move along the ground according to their kinds. And God saw that it was good.

Genesis 1:24-25

The pattern, whereby God creates creatures to fill the arenas he has made, is repeated. On day 5, as the birds and the fish filled the spaces God made on day 2, so, on day 6, God creates the creatures to fill the land space he made on day 3.

The living creatures God made on day 6 are divided into three categories: livestock, creatures that move along the ground and wild animals. But all these creatures come from the land. Wenham suggests that essentially these categories could be described as domestic, wild and small animals. The last named could be translated "creeping things" and refers to mice, reptiles, insects and any other little creatures that keep close to the ground.[12] It is perhaps worth noting that reptiles (and that of course includes snakes) are all created by God: but we'll come to the relevance of that later. Essentially, every living thing that lives on the earth was created by God. The suggestion here is that God didn't create

12 Wenham, *Genesis 1-15*, p25

43

them 'out of nothing' but 'from the earth'. We also need to note that once again there is the clear differentiation of these living creatures into their various 'kinds'. The fact that this is repeated so often is surely more than simply a poetic device but, rather, a means of telling the reader that God set boundaries between the animals to keep them in their separate 'compartments'. And the way that God created the animals means that animals do not naturally reproduce with animals outside their own species.

Have you ever thought about that? Cats don't seek a dog for a mate; pigs don't look to sheep. But each category, or kind, knows to seek a mate from its own kind. It is inbuilt into their make-up. The divine mandate to be fruitful is missing from this section but I think is incorporated into the divine command which follows the final created species in verse 28. Scientists estimate there to be something like 8.7 million different species of life on earth of which 1-2 million are animals. Again, the breadth of diversity is astounding!

> Okay, so, time for a challenge, if you're up for it? Set your timer for 60 seconds and write down as many animals as you can think of: let's see how many of the 1-2 million you know!

However, even within species there is an amazing variety. Take dogs for example: with help from intentional breeding by human beings (who we'll come back to in a moment), isn't it incredible that dogs can be as large as Great Danes yet as small as Chihuahuas. All are dogs as distinct from any other kind of animal, but *so* different. Interesting too that, right from the outset, some animals were described as 'livestock', made for a particular purpose, whereas others were wild. Now this flies in the face of the evolutionary thesis. And it has to be said that science has proven there is certainly some degree of evolution of species over time. But, as far as I know, the famous illusive 'missing link' confirming the suggestion that humans evolved from apes, remains just that: 'missing'. And according to the essence of the creation narrative it will continue to remain so. I realise that what I am saying here may be somewhat contentious in certain quarters. Again, the essence of the Bible is not, I would dare to say, majorly concerned with addressing our scientific concerns. It is much keener to draw our eyes to the amazing Creator God who spoke all these beautiful, crazy, colourful, comical, creatures into being and stood back and said once more: that it was good v25.

When we read verse 26 onwards, we arrive at the creation of the most sophisticated animal made by God. The way the account is set out takes God's creativity to a whole new level. The next species to be brought into play are of a totally new order from any animal that has come before. Stand by for the climax of the creation account![13]

> Then God said, "Let us make mankind in our image, in our likeness,
> so that they may rule over the fish in the sea and the birds in the sky,
> over the livestock and all the wild animals, and over all the creatures that
> move along the ground."
> So God created mankind in his own image,
> in the image of God he created him:

13 Wenham, *Genesis 1-15*, p27

male and female he created them.

God blessed them and said to them, "Be fruitful and increase in number; fill the earth and subdue it. Rule over the fish in the sea and the birds in the sky and over every living creature that moves on the ground.

Genesis 1:26-28

THE MAKING OF MANKIND

Now you may remember me suggesting that the creation account (thus far) was a little like the stage being prepared in a theatre ready for a new play to be performed. The climax to the operation would be the arrival of the actors on the stage. Well, *this* is the moment. The scene is set and, with these verses, we are about to be introduced to the stars of the show. The actors enter the stage as mankind makes its first appearance. These verses are probably some of the most studied, analysed and discussed verses in the whole Bible; understandably so as *this* is the moment our own stories begin. I doubt very much that you will read much that is entirely original (if anything) in what follows but let's take a look anyway.

To begin with, did you notice the subtle change in the creative process of this verse?

So far, we've read: "Let there be" or: "Let the land/water produce…". We've seen it in verses: 3, 6, 9, 11, 14, 20, 24. But when we come to creation of human beings, the creative process becomes truly personal as we read: "Let *us* make mankind in *our* image, in *our* likeness." Genesis 1:26.

That change alone notifies us of the incredible nature of this next level of creation that sets mankind apart from all that has come before. With the creation of mankind, we are witnessing the creation of a species that God is actively invested in. This is in a way that we have not witnessed before. Not only this though, this species, unlike all the others we have encountered, uniquely reflects the Creator!

What we are reading here is something truly remarkable:

Then God said, "Let us make mankind in our image, in our likeness."

Genesis 1:26

What a breath-taking verse this is and it's one that raises so many questions. Two in particular are:

1) Who does God mean when he speaks of "us" and "our"?
2) What is meant by mankind being made in God's "image" and "likeness"?

Let's take the first question first: who is the "us" and "our" of this verse?

One suggestion is that God is here addressing his heavenly court (that is, his angels - although as yet they have not made an appearance in the story). Support for this view comes from other places in the Old Testament like Psalm 82:1, and also Isaiah 6:8.

A second popular suggestion is that we are reading here of God, speaking as the triune God, declaring that human beings are to be made in some way like Him in his three-in-oneness. Wenham notes though, that: 'it is now universally admitted that this was not what the plural meant to the original author.'[14]

Others have suggested this is an example of a plural of majesty; the English royal "we" referring to the fullness of God within the God-head.[15] Still others suggest this is a plural of self-deliberation.[16]

> So, let me pause afresh and ask you the question: What do you think? Who would you say is the "us" here?

Okay, now let me tell you the answer..... Oh if only I could! The reality is that we don't know for sure.

What we do know is that on the sixth day, when everything was ready, God announced the time had come for the creation of the true climax of His creative works; the making of beings which God describes as being made "in our image, in our likeness."

And that leads us to our second question, what exactly is meant by this incredible description? To begin, as we read a little further, we hear the *reason*, the "so that," for their creation:

"Let us make mankind in our image, in our likeness,
so that they may rule over the fish in the sea and the birds in the sky,
over the livestock and all the wild animals, and over all the creatures that
move along the ground."

14   Wenham, *Genesis 1-15*, p27
15   *Ibid* p28
16   *Ibid* p28

Whatever else this imaging of God means, by making mankind in God's image and likeness, they are able to "rule over" the other created creatures that God had made and hitherto not named. Just as God rules over the creation he has made, so mankind is here delegated the rule/dominion over the other creatures that God has made.

This then begs the question what does God's rule over creation look like in comparison with mankind's? For a start, God made the other creatures from the earth instructing them to be fruitful. He provided them with vegetation to eat and gave them the means to multiply. Mankind really can't emulate an awful lot of this save ensuring that there is sufficient vegetation for the animals to feed on and ensuring there is an environment to enable God's instructions to be carried out. Thus, any sense of "rule" here pertains to mankind providing care and provision for the other creatures as opposed to any sense of dominance.

So, if mankind is to rule over, is that the extent to which they image God? My own thought here is that the 'ruling over' is something that mankind is to do (part of their function), *because* they are made in God's image (somehow sharing something of the essence of who God is) not simply to complete it. If that is right, then to image God and to be in his likeness requires further consideration.

This again begs the question: What is meant by mankind being made in God's "image" and "likeness"? Biblical scholars have debated the exact meaning of these words for many years. Wenham helpfully summarises the arguments saying: "The strongest case has been made for the view that the divine image makes man God's vice-regent on earth. Because man is God's representative, his life is sacred: every assault on man is an affront to the creator and merits the ultimate penalty (Genesis 9:5-6)."[17] But I can't help feeling there is more to it than that.

Jumping forward again into the New Testament we find an interesting clue in a letter written by the Apostle Paul to the church in Colossae.

In Colossians 1:15 we read this written about Jesus:

> 'The Son (Jesus) is the image of the invisible God, the firstborn over all creation. For in him all things were created: things in heaven and on earth, visible and invisible, whether thrones or powers or rulers or authorities; all things have been created through him and for him.'
> Colossians 1:15-16

Paul makes a similar claim in his letter to the church in Corinth (2 Corinthians 4:4). So how might this help?

Firstly, we are told here that God is 'invisible', so being made in his image and likeness cannot suggest that we simply look (visibly) like him.

Secondly, Jesus, the Son of God, *reveals* God. Somehow, as a human being, Jesus shows us what, or maybe better '*who*' God is. When we see his image, we actually get to see what God is like. Now, to my mind, this is what that very first human was called upon to do. When God said: Let us make mankind in

17   *Ibid* p31-32

our image, in our likeness, I believe God was essentially setting forth his creative plans for this species, unlike any other that He'd made. These humans were supposed to make known the invisible God. In all ways, they were to make His invisible self, known. That was their mandate: to be like God. And something went wrong! We'll soon find out what. But the amazing claim Paul makes in his letters is that when Jesus appeared, he fulfilled the original *human* mandate too, and therefore shows us not only what God is like, but also what we, humans, are supposed to be like: we're supposed to be like God!

So God created mankind in his own image,
in the image of God he created him;
male and female he created them.

Genesis 1:27

This verse acts as a summary statement similar to ones seen before like v7, 21. The key word, repeated three times, is the word 'created'. In no uncertain terms the writer wants us to know that *God* made mankind, and He made them in His image. Maybe as a prelude to the more detailed account of 'how' he did it that we find in Genesis 2, the verse suggests that God made 'him' first, one solitary human being who would represent the species he would begin. But then from that 'him' would come forth 'them': humanity as male and female to enable this potentiality of multiplication to proceed.

This verse has other things to tell us about the nature of humans too.

THE NATURE OF HUMANITY

Here we come across something we have already met, the combination of the oneness of God coupled to his mysterious plurality. When the Genesis account began, we noted the peculiar way we were introduced to God right at the outset of Genesis 1: One God yet someone seen as God the Creator, but having a Spirit who is certainly *one* with him yet somehow *other* to him. And then there was the Word of God who was of course God's word speaking creation into being. Yet, He is found in the beginning of John's Gospel to be somehow separate to Him. Here we read that humanity is created as him (singular pointing to our 'oneness'); yet it is only as male *and* female (plural suggesting our essential 'community') that God is truly imaged by them.

I'm aware that some suggest the 'three-ness' of God is imaged by understanding mankind to be a tripartite being having a body (our flesh), our soul (our mind, will and emotions) and our human spirit.[18] There is certainly biblical support for these three aspects of the human being.[19] However, the complex and unique three-ness of God: as Father, Son and Holy Spirit is seen in their separate 'persons' in their own right, not simply aspects of one person. The early church-fathers took pains to hammer this out as they sought to articulate the uniqueness of the plurality within the Godhead – three persons - whilst simultaneously maintaining His absolute oneness (the Trinity).[20] However, the plurality this

18 R.Hawkey, *Healing the Human Spirit*, Chichester, West Sussex: New Wine Press, 2004, p12-13
19 See for example 1 Thessalonians 5:23
20 G. McFarlane, *Why Do You Believe what you believe about the Holy Spirit?*, Carlisle, Cumbria, Paternoster Press, 1998, p59-63

verse, Genesis 1:27, seems to emphasize is the plurality of sexes: they are separate, different, and yet both necessary *together*. God is imaged in the creation of humanity. The fulness of that imaging is only seen when humanity is created as community, as male *and* female. And that plurality enables humans to undertake a further aspect of their creation mandate:

God blessed them and said to them, "Be fruitful and increase in number; fill the earth and subdue it. Rule over the fish in the sea and the birds in the sky and over every living creature that moves on the ground." Genesis 1:28

Now that a being like him has been created, God addresses them directly: God speaks 'to them'. There is, therefore, the beginnings of a 'relationship' between God the Creator and mankind the created. We also see that God's desire for mankind is entirely positive. They are to 'Be fruitful and increase in number; fill the earth and subdue it.'

God doesn't need to go into detail, they'll get the hang of it! There is a huge earth set in place; it is perfectly set up to allow life to flourish and this first human pair have the exciting adventure before them of exploring it and settling in it. They are to increase in number through their sexual reproduction and, as they grow in number and spread out upon the earth, they are to rule over the created world. God has put them in charge. So, they are to: 'Rule over the fish in the sea and the birds in the sky and over every living creature that moves on the ground.' God has made a vast array of species of different kinds to inhabit the waters, the skies and to move along the ground and He has delegated His rule over them to humans! Wow!

But God isn't finished yet:

> Then God said, "I give you every seed-bearing plant on the face of the whole earth and every tree that has fruit with seed in it. They will be yours for food. And to all the beasts of the earth and all the birds in the sky and all the creatures that move along the ground – everything that has the breath of life in it – I give every green plant for food. And it was so.
>
> Genesis 1:29-30

Reading this I can't help but think that things were very different way back when. For a start there is no hint here that humanity's diet would involve eating anything other than every seed-bearing plant on the face of the whole earth and every tree that has fruit with seed in it. Seemingly, for both animals and humans, their original diet was entirely vegetarian! For a God who delights in giving life, it's perfectly then reasonable to think that the death of a creature would be anathema! Which makes the apparent bloodlust for sacrifices that we find in only the third book of the Bible seem somewhat incomprehensible. What could possibly have caused such a dramatic turnaround? We'll come to that soon enough.

When God saw all that he had made, this time he pronounces it: "very good". And there was evening, and there was morning – the sixth day. Genesis 1:31

God stands back and looks, not just at the work of day 6, but on all that he had made, and it wasn't just good, it was *very* good.

In the six days of creation, we have progressed from 'formless and empty' to the earth teeming with life and possibilities. God has made beings like Himself, and has given them the mandate to care for his incredible creation. There is no hint of death, disease or disorder. The whole picture to this point is one of an incredible garden paradise and a journey of discovery that would be the envy of any would-be backpacker or adventurer. So, as we turn to Genesis chapter 2 we read a concluding statement:

> Thus the heavens and the earth were completed in all their vast array.
>
> Genesis 2:1

The scene is set for our story to really begin. The curtains of creation are drawn back; the main actors have entered the stage; it's time for the first act.

2.
GENESIS 2
The Seventh Day

By the seventh day God had finished the work he had been doing; so on the seventh day he rested from all his work. Then God blessed the seventh day and made it holy, because on it he rested from all the work of creating that he had done.

Genesis 2:2-3

Now to my mind, this would be the place to end the first chapter of Genesis, as opposed to beginning the second. This is the account of... that begins v4 would seem to me to be a logical first verse of a new section. But, as I mentioned earlier, the chapter and verse breaks that we have in our Bibles were not part of the original manuscript but only added later to help us find our way around.[21] This would be one of the places that our helpful editor might not have been so helpful.

21 Robert Estienne (Robert Stephanus) was the first to number the verses within each chapter, his verse numbers entering printed editions in 1551 (New Testament) and 1571 (Hebrew Bible).

THE UNFINISHED SEVENTH DAY

Back to the text there is something glaringly missing from this seventh day that concluded the previous six days of creation. There is no: 'And there was evening and there was morning – the seventh day.' Rather, the seventh day is left open. It's like the day isn't fully over just yet.

There's another obvious difference here too. On the seventh day there's no action. God doesn't say: "Let there be" anything, because we are told God had finished the work he had been doing. So, with the creation of mankind, God had reached the climax of his creative plans. It was finished. And, as we read in 1:31, when God saw all that he had made, it was very good.

I guess the story could have stopped there: Creation done, mankind in place to care for it. God taking time out. The Bible could have been a much shorter book! But there is still plenty more to come. We've seen before how God 'blessed' aspects of creation, setting them off with his approval (1:22, 28), but on day 7 it is not living creatures that he blesses but the very seventh day itself: Then God blessed the seventh day and made it holy... v3.

Now "holy" is one of those words that we often bandy about, but we probably understand different things by it. A definition I like is that it means something, or someone, being 'set apart' or given over for the purposes/intentions of God. In other words, it's His! Given that we said earlier that there is no closing formulae used to close the seventh day, it says to me that what follows is essentially all about God: the fact that he 'blessed' this day, says to me that what follows in Genesis 2 onwards is to be the story of God. This creation is all about Him! And, ultimately, the creation itself will acknowledge that because God's blessing lies upon it.

But there is more to this of course. We read earlier how human beings were made by God to "image" Him in relation to Creation. They were to make Him known. Well, in this verse, one of the ways that they are to do so is by emulating this pattern of living and working. God works for six days in completing his Creation then he rests. So too there is a pattern here for humans to follow; to work in managing this incredible creation and ruling over it as God would have them do but also building in a day a week to cease from this activity. That is a day to be refreshed through resting and refocusing on the one who set this day apart for Himself. Later in the story we'll see just how important this seven-day pattern is but for now the section concludes with a very powerful word: 'done'. It is finished! We might hear this same idea later in the Bible story! But, for now, the finishing of creation is only really the beginning of what is to come.

As we turn to Genesis 2:4 onwards, our focus is drawn back to God's image bearers who will continue the story.

However, before we turn to that, I wonder how you've found this opening chapter? What was the writer's intentions in writing it? How does reading this chapter impact your faith?

I heard someone dismissing the Genesis account as a 'fairy story' the other day which saddened me greatly. Far from being a 'fairy story,' as I read Genesis 1, I marvel at the profound way that it introduces the most incredible concepts and questions that mankind has, questions relating to our formation and purpose, in ways that are simple enough for young minds to understand yet complex enough for the most intellectual boffins to spend their lives trying to unpack. In my view, the purpose of this chapter is not even to try and answer our 'how' and 'when' questions but to tell a bigger story: the 'why' story.

However, the more I've thought about it, the more I think it might actually be less even than about the 'why' of it all and more about the 'who'! When I read this chapter, I read of an incredibly powerful God who only has to speak and stars and galaxies appear. I read of a God who delights in creativity, in colour, in design; a generous God who over supplies. A God who makes human beings to be exactly like him, creatures that he can speak to and have a relationship with. A God who knows the value of creative work but who also knows that we need rest too. In fact, I read of a God who wants us to rest first then to work *out of* that rest, then to rest again. This is a God who wants us to join him in delighting in the works of our hands. A God who is strangely One God, yet a community of three completely interdependent Persons in perfect harmony with Himself yet longing to share this oneness with others who are like Him. A God who longs to bless but has boundaries and structures that exaggerate this blessing. To my mind, this story of how it all began is truly inspiring and such a joy to read. So important is it that we set off on the right path that our writer then gives us a second bite of the cherry. When we turn to Genesis 2, we get a second chance to see all this played out. Viewing creation from a different angle, let us continue our Prologue adventure!

This is the account of the heavens and the earth when they were created, when the LORD God made the earth and the heavens. Genesis 2:4

This verse reads something like a heading introducing the next section of the story. And despite it sounding as though it is simply going to go back over the same material as we read in chapter 1, we will soon find that it is actually much more focused on the lives of the first human, Adam, and his family.

THE ADAM FAMILY

The section begins by focusing on Adam's territory (2:5-25); this is followed by one of the most tragic stories ever told which explains how, or perhaps better *why*, Adam had to leave this territory (3:1-24). The story, perhaps unsurprisingly given what we've said about 'sevens' previously, seems to break down into seven scenes:[22]

Scene 1) 2:5-17
God the sole actor: Adam present but uninvolved

Scene 2) 2:18-25
God main actor: Adam has a minor role: Eve present but uninvolved

Scene 3) 3:1-5
Dialogue between Eve and the snake

---

22 Wenham, *Genesis 1-15*, p50

Scene 4) 3:6-8
Adam and Eve centre stage

Scene 5) 3:9-13
Dialogue between God, Adam and Eve

Scene 6) 3:14-21
God main actor: Adam has a minor role: Eve and the snake
present but uninvolved

Scene 7) 3:22-24
God the sole actor: Adam present but uninvolved

This type of careful structuring appears often in Biblical texts and it's so helpful in drawing the reader's eye to the critical centre point of the passage: this is often where the most important point is reached. More than that, each scene carefully mirrors its counterpart: scene 1 balances scene 7, scene 2 balances scene 6, scene 3 balances scene 5. Again, our writer is very carefully and deliberately organising the way he writes his account.

Before we dive into the text though, we might pause to ask ourselves the question: what sort of literature are we reading here? The technical term for this is 'genre'. So, for example if we were to read a newspaper, we would find ourselves reading different genres without really thinking about it. We know instinctively how to read cartoons as clever and funny ways of making comment without truly believing that dogs can converse with humans. We know how to read obituaries as summaries of someone's life but generally written to be as positive as possible.

We read lists of TV programmes to gain information but read the summaries of them knowing that these are opinions being given. Similarly, we might see Editorials where opinions are freely expressed alongside Articles purportedly giving us the facts of a situation. You get the gist of it. We are used to reading the journals of our age, but how do we interpret a story written so long ago in a culture that we are entirely unfamiliar with? Bible commentators discuss this sort of question in fine detail. If you were to read their comments on these chapters you would note that they contrast this Biblical account with other non-biblical stories that archaeologists have discovered from other ancient cultures. It's very interesting how many similarities exist between these ancient stories too. But does that mean that they are all drawing on a common history? Or does it mean that one story is written to critique another? These are important questions that I don't intend to comment on further here.

The thoughts and reflections that follow are simply my observations on what the Bible says, taken very much at face value.

> So, before we proceed, how about you? How will you read these verses? What genre do you think you are reading here, and how do you think it should be interpreted? Maybe the difficulty in knowing how to answer these questions should make us cautious in how we do seek to interpret what we read!

With those questions in mind, let's dive in and see what Genesis 2 has in store for us!

Now no shrub had yet appeared on the earth and no plant had yet sprung up, for the LORD God had not sent rain on the earth and there was no one to work the ground, but streams came up from the earth and watered the whole surface of the ground.

Genesis 2:5-6

WELL-WATERED GROUND

As we pick up the story, it seems here to be *before* God made the vegetation, which if you've being paying attention, was said to take place on the third day. However, as this chapter follows on from Genesis 1, we might expect that it isn't going to repeat the same information verbatim. Rather, it will draw out certain aspects of what has already been set out to make the points the writer wishes to concentrate on.

As I mentioned before, our interpretation of these verses is a little hampered by the fact that we are reading a translation of the original text and thus what we have is already an interpretation. Every time a translation is made from one language into another, linguists have to make decisions about grammar and word use as to how best to make that transfer as accurate as possible. However, by its very nature, this calls for judgement and thereby interpretation. For example, in these two verses the original text included three different geographic terms: 'plain', 'earth' and 'land' as well as two terms for vegetation: 'shrub' and 'plant'. So, one of our questions might involve trying to discern if there is a reason for using these different terms or is this an example of Hebrew parallelism?[23] According to Wenham,

23 Hebrew Parallelism is found throughout the Bible and involves the writer

'earth' is a broad term for the land surface of the planet whereas 'land' comprises part of the earth. Over against the cultivated land stands the open uncultivated 'plain'.[24]

Wenham therefore translates these verses as follows:

> No shrub of the plain had yet grown in the earth, nor had any plant of the plain yet sprung up, because the LORD God had not made it rain on the earth and there was no man to till the land. But the fresh water ocean used to rise from the earth and water the whole surface of the land.[25]

By using this more detailed translation, the verse may be seen to be making a specific point that is easily lost on us. Wenham suggests that Genesis 2:5 is distinguishing two types of land: open, uncultivated "plain" or "field," the wilderness fit only for animal grazing, and the dusty "land" where agriculture is possible with irrigation and human effort. Similarly, the difference between "shrub" and "plant" seems to lie in whether they may be eaten or not.[26] It has therefore been suggested that this verse is actually quite humancentric, in that it is describing the struggle that humans will subsequently face to bring more "plain" under cultivation and conversely to prevent land being reduced to "plain" which will be outlined in Genesis 3:17-18.[27]

---

using this poetic device in different ways. The basic approach is to write the same thought in a slightly different way in the following line, or occasionally with antithetic parallelism to write the subsequent line to express an opposite thought.

24 Wenham, *Genesis 1-15*, p58
25 *Ibid*, p44
26 *Ibid*, p58
27 *Ibid* p58

Furthermore, the abundant water supply described in v6 seems inadequate to create vegetation without the introduction of humans to 'till the land'. Thus, instead of reading these verses as repeating earlier descriptions of God's creative process, they seem to form an introduction to the human story that begins to be told in the next verse. God has created a magnificent world but, unless mankind is there to tend it, the best will not be brought out of it. So, verses 5 and 6, far from repeating details of creation, are maybe better read as a prelude and introduction to the human story which is what the writer wishes to focus on.

Then the LORD God formed a man from the dust of the ground and breathed into his nostrils the breath of life, and the man became a living being.

Genesis 2:7

THE FORMING OF A MAN

Like Genesis 1:26, when the story described the making of a human being, there is much to be considered in this verse. The preceding verses have drawn our attention to the close connection humans have to the earth, now we find man is created from the very dust of the earth.[28] Our English translations miss out on the Hebrew play on words that so closely relates the man to the dust he came from. But the man's relationship to the earth

28 It is apparent that human beings share many similarities with the chemical components of the earth. But the explanation of God fashioning a human being into the complex beings we are simply from the dust of the earth gives us some ideas as to what the writer is doing here. This is not a detailed scientific explanation of the creation of humanity but an explanation of the essentials we need to know in understanding our story. Our human existence is completely linked to the physical world we live in, yet our life is granted to us by a gift of God (he breathes life into us).

is paramount. He is created from it; his role is to cultivate and care for it (2:5); and when he finally dies (though of course we don't know this yet) he will return to it (3:19).

We read that God 'formed a man'; other translations say 'shaped a man' a word generally associated with the way a potter shapes clay into a pot or some such vessel. This is a concept that is common throughout the Bible and used not just in the formation of humans but also of animals (Genesis 2:19) and even the dry land (Psalm 95:5). Some of the prophets use the same word to describe the way God shapes or forms history (Isaiah 22:11) or even how God shapes a human character or a people group to fulfil a particular role in that history (Isaiah 43:21). But the idea that mankind was created from the dust is also a common feature of the Bible story (see for example Job 10:9). This idea is also seen in other ancient non-biblical creation narratives such as the Gilgamesh Epic. But it's one thing to shape a pot, it's a completely different thing to bring that 'pot' to life! Here we read God 'breathed into his nostrils the breath of life'.

This word 'breathed' is similar to a word used when someone gives a fire a good blow to help rekindle its embers. The prophet Ezekiel uses the same idea in describing life being blown into dry bones to bring them back to life (Ezekiel 37). Literally, this verse affirms that it was God who brought this vessel to life and made him breathe so that the man became a "living creature". That is to say that mankind owes our very existence, our very *lives* to the God who made us. To think that we would do better by living without any reference to him is thus shown to be completely ridiculous (21st-Century Western World beware). So here we have a man, made from the very dust of the earth, who has a material substance to him. Yet that isn't all he is. He is *alive*, given life from the very breath of God. Remembering what we said elsewhere about the commonality in meaning between breath, wind and *spirit*, maybe we should also say that this man is a spiritual creature. Mankind is that wonderful meeting place of dust and breath, of physical and spiritual; the crowning aspect of God's creation and the very epicentre of the story that the Bible is about to unfold.[29]

Having established that humans are essential for the flourishing of the planet, and closely allied to its very make up, the writer now continues his story.

> **Now the LORD God had planted a garden in the east, in Eden; and there he put the man he had formed.**
> Genesis 2:8

GARDENERS WORLD

So, having created the man, God now has an idyllic place in mind in which he might begin to live. Biblical commentators suggest that the meaning of 'garden' here is something equivalent to an unenclosed space suitable for cultivation. It has connotations of

---

29 I can't help referencing John 20:19-23 where we read that when Jesus rose from the dead he somehow entered the locked room where his disciples were hiding for fear of the Jewish leaders who had just ordered Jesus' crucifixion. He showed them his wounds so they knew it was really him. Then he did an interesting thing – he breathed on them and said: "Receive the Holy Spirit." I can't help thinking that John who, as we've seen earlier, seems to be telling the story of Jesus as a new start for humanity, is showing how the death and resurrection of Jesus really does signal a new start for humanity: this breathing on them is like a counterpart to Genesis 2:7.

a royal park, a paradise for the man to enjoy and be safe in. And now we are given a specific reference: this garden is in Eden, in the East. Which begs the question: East of where?

Later in the Bible story we will find that God's centre of reference will become a small area of land known as Canaan. So one thought is that this area, known as Eden, is east of that land. We can hold that thought for the time being. But what is significant about it being in the East?

At the beginning of our journey into Genesis we saw that God began his work of creation with the declaration, "Let there be light" Genesis 1:3. God is the light bringer. And, of course, the sun rises in the East. So, one idea is that somehow the place where the light rises is the place where God is found – the author of light. Given that it was God himself who is described here as the gardener, maybe it's not too much of a stretch to understand this verse as alluding to Eden as the place where God is most fully known to dwell. This idea might be further supported by a consideration of the place where the man is to dwell, Eden.

In Isaiah 51:3 we read: The LORD will surely comfort Zion and will look with compassion on all her ruins; he will make her deserts like Eden, her wastelands like the garden of the LORD.

A similar thought is expressed in Ezekiel 31:9. So, this verse seems to be suggesting that the man is placed in God's own garden paradise, to live with Him and enjoy His presence and His space.

We'll hear more about God's gardening skills in just a moment in the verses that follow. But first I just want to take us on a bit of a detour.

Can you remember who it was that first encountered the risen Jesus after his death and burial, and who she thought he was? In John 20:11ff we read these wonderful words:

> Now Mary stood outside the tomb crying. As she wept, she bent over to look into the tomb and saw two angels in white, seated where Jesus' body had been, one at the head and the other at the foot. They asked her, "Woman, why are you crying?" "They have taken my Lord away," she said, "and I don't know where they have put him." At this, she turned around and saw Jesus standing there, but she did not realise that it was Jesus.
>
> He asked her, "Woman, why are you crying? Who is it you are looking for?"
>
> *Thinking he was the gardener,* she said, "Sir, if you have carried him away, tell me where you have put him, and I will get him." Jesus said to her, "Mary." She turned toward him and cried out in Aramaic, "Rabboni!" (which means "Teacher"). (Italics added!)

I absolutely love these verses! Firstly, because it's a woman who first recognizes the risen Jesus (we'll understand more of the significance of that when we look at Genesis 3). But I love it too that when Mary first sees the risen Jesus, she doesn't initially recognize him but instead thinks he's the *gardener*!

When humanity, here in the guise of Mary, is reintroduced to God's risen Son, Jesus, her first thought is that she is encountering 'the gardener'. And I want to say: *indeed* she is! Just as Adam began his days in God's garden paradise of Eden, so the resurrection of Jesus allows us to meet the gardener once more. When we believe in Jesus, *then* we can re-enter paradise. But that is to jump well ahead in our story. Let us return to the original Eden and find out a little more about God's gardening prowess:

> The LORD God made all kinds of trees grow out of the ground – trees that were pleasing to the eye and good for food. In the middle of the garden were the tree of life and the tree of the knowledge of good and evil.
>
> Genesis 2:9

TWO SPECIAL TREES

Once more the absolute abundance of God's generosity is our starting point. God made all kinds of trees grow out of the ground. Not just one type or a few types but *multitudes*. It is estimated that today there are something like 60,000 different species of tree in our world; we'll see in a moment how, originally, there were at least two more! Not only were these trees to provide food for the man but they were pleasing to the eye. When God sets up this garden paradise for the man He has made, He wants him to totally love it!

Especially, in the middle of the garden, we are told that there were two very special trees: the tree of life and the tree of the knowledge of good and evil.

Now again, there is a partial parallel to this in other ancient, non-biblical creation stories. The Gilgamesh Epic, for example, also includes a plant which seemed to confer eternal youth. But there is no parallel that I am aware of for the tree of the knowledge of good and evil. So, we need to give very careful consideration to what is meant by these two trees and why they appear at the centre of the garden.

Before we do, it would be worth noting that references to 'a tree of life' appear elsewhere in the Bible story, mainly in the setting of giving wisdom. For example, in a chapter that is extolling the virtues of wisdom, we read this:

> Long life is in her right hand; in her left hand are riches and honour.
> Her ways are pleasant ways and all her paths are peace.
> She is a *tree of life* to those who take hold of her; those who hold her fast will be blessed.
>
> Proverbs 3:16-18.

Similarly, in Proverbs 11:30 we read:

> The fruit of the righteous is a *tree of life*, and the one who is wise saves lives.

The point seems to be that whoever finds wisdom, or walks in the path of wisdom, lives a full life, the sort of life that God initially had in mind for the man who has direct access to a fruit tree bearing life.

The book of Psalms also begins with an introductory Psalm, Psalm 1, which similarly suggests that the person:

> whose delight is in the law of the LORD, and who meditates on his law day and night... is like a tree planted by streams of water, which yields its fruit in season and who leaf does not wither – whatever they do prospers.
>
> Psalm 1:2-3.

By combining these ideas, we get the picture that whoever lives God's way, is the person who lives wisely; and *that* person is going to live the fullest, most fruitful of lives. The symbolism of the tree of life is that it is offering the man life in all its fulness. And its fruit is there for the taking.

But there is also a second tree!

If the first tree seems to be offering the man 'wisdom' that leads to life, the second tree is offering 'knowledge'. They are, of course, not the same thing.[30] And if the first tree offered life, we'll soon find out that the fruit of the second tree offers only its opposite (Genesis 2:17). So, does God want to keep the man ignorant? Does He want him to have no knowledge of good and evil? If we are not to completely misunderstand the rationale that this tree represents, we need to give this matter careful consideration!

> But before we do that, time for you to do some thinking first. What do you think these two trees symbolise?

The clue to unpacking the second strange tree may be found in Ezekiel 28. That chapter describes how the King of Tyre was

---

30 A dictionary defines **Knowledge** as the information you have learned, while **wisdom** is the ability to use that **knowledge in a** profound way. **Wisdom** goes beyond learning facts and includes making sense of those facts.

expelled from Eden because of his pride, claiming himself to be as wise as a god (Ezekiel 28:2,6).[31] Thus, it is not the acquisition of knowledge that is wrong, indeed that pursuit seems to be part of the very fabric of what makes human beings like God. However, if that knowledge should lead to them becoming "puffed up" with self-importance so that they come to think of themselves as somehow on a par with God (as the King of Tyre had apparently done), then that knowledge would inexorably lead to their demise – hence Genesis 2:17. To pursue knowledge with a view to being somehow autonomous from God their creator is actually the opposite to the starting point for wisdom which Proverbs asserts to be the fear for the LORD (Proverbs 1:7).[32]

THE ESSENTIAL CHOICE

So, it could be said that here, at the epicentre of the paradise garden, God has provided the man with the most fundamental and basic choices: will he continue to feast upon wisdom, here described as the fruit of the tree of life, symbolising his willing submission to his creatureliness, putting his trust in God to be blessed with the fullest of lives, or will he rather choose to reject that place and instead feed on the tree of the knowledge of good and evil. By doing so he would be asserting his desire for independence, stating in effect that despite being created by God, owing his very existence to him, he thinks he is better off

31 It's not my remit to try and explain that particular chapter here, but I would strongly suggest you have a read of it for yourself!

32 In case we misunderstand the meaning of this phrase, 'The fear of the LORD' is best understood to be a loving reverence for God that includes submission to his lordship and to the commands of his word.

being his own master. This is, in effect, the assertion: I want to do it my way. (Now where have I heard that before?!)

The choice is thus made clear: this has led many to ask why God made that choice available in the first place? Why plant the second tree? I have the utmost respect for those who do ask that question. Seeking knowledge, as we've just said, isn't wrong in and of itself. But before we face the question, I must stress that the motive behind it needs to be carefully considered! Remembering that wisdom begins with the fear of the LORD, if anyone is coming to this question with any degree of human arrogance I would suggest a strong note of caution. The essential choice that these two trees demonstrate is a subtle but vital choice that actually sums up the whole human experience. This is why I believe we have it here so early on in the prologue of Genesis 1 to 3.

The choice is this: will we put our trust in the God who gave us life and receive the fulness of life that can only be found in him; or will we seek our own autonomy, thinking we know best. There is a stark consequence of this latter position that we'll hear about in a verse or two. But that is the fundamental question each and every human being at some stage in our lives needs to face: do I put my trust in God or do I put my trust in myself? You cannot have it both ways. So, why would God place this choice at the centre of the space he created for the man to live in? I have heard it argued that without giving mankind this fundamental choice, God could not fully enter into a genuine relationship with the humans He created. Unless they had the very real choice to turn away from Him then the relationship would not have been a genuine one. Hence, God has to allow for the eventuality that the humans He made might think they could turn away from Him, even be better off without Him. The choice has to be genuine even if the outcome could prove to be potentially catastrophic. The choice had to be made available or the creatures God had made would not truly be made in his image.

> Of course, we too essentially face the same choice, although our starting point is reversed. Adam and Eve began life with God and then had to consider whether to continue to trust him or opt out. We find ourselves adrift from God and then have to choose whether to trust in God and opt back in. (We'll find out why when we get to Genesis 3). We also need to decide how we will live our lives. Will we seek the tree of life, that which begins with the fear of the Lord, or will we simply seek knowledge that seemingly puts us in charge of our own destiny but in so doing rejects the very one who gave us life? I wonder, which tree is predominant in how you are living your life right now?

Returning to Genesis, as if to allow us time and space to consider this question, we have a pause in the text, a detour perhaps to let the vital importance of the trees sink in. Before we return to the trees, we are called to consider how they might be watered.

A river watering the garden flowed from Eden; from there it was separated into four headwaters. The name of the first is the Pishon; it winds through the entire land of Havilah, where there is gold. (The gold of that land is good; aromatic resin and onyx are also there.) The name of the second river is the

Gihon; it winds through the entire land of Cush. The name of the third river is the Tigris; it runs along the east side of Ashur. And the fourth river is the Euphrates.   Genesis 2:10-14

A WATERY INTERLUDE

Now it has to be admitted that these verses add an interesting interlude into the account. Some commentators suggest that they come from a separate source. Our understanding of them is somewhat confused by the fact that some of the names mentioned are still known to us, some are not. So, what's going on here? What are these verses telling us?

We begin with the phrase: a river watering the garden flowed from Eden. Now I suggested earlier that the idea of the garden paradise of Eden might symbolise the very epicentre of God's presence on earth. Many ancient cultures, Israel included, constructed a temple to symbolise the focal point of God's presence among them. As we read on in the Bible story, we find that some time after leaving the sanctuary of Eden, God called on a small tribe of people, the Jews, to be the means of fulfilling His saving plans for his created masterpiece. He initially instructed them to build a portable temple or tabernacle to represent His presence among them (the book of Exodus wonderfully describes this process for the Israelites). But, once the people had settled into the land God had in mind for them, it was King David's son Solomon who then built a magnificent temple for God in the nation's capital Jerusalem. However, this incredible structure was eventually destroyed by the Babylonians in 587/6 BC when large numbers of Jews were taken into captivity in Babylon and Jerusalem was sacked. The prophet Ezekiel was later given incredible visions of the restoration of the temple. This was to give hope to the exiles that God wasn't finished with his people and that he would bring them home. Now the reason for my historical detour comes in Ezekiel 47. There we read some interesting details that remind me of what we are reading here. In Ezekiel's vision we read that water was coming forth from the temple:

> The man (Ezekiel's angelic guide) brought me back to the entrance to the temple, and I saw water coming out from under the threshold of the temple toward the east (for the temple faced east). The water was coming down from under the south side of the temple, south of the altar. He then brought me out through the north gate and led me around the outside to the outer gate facing east, and the water was flowing from the south side.
>
> Ezekiel 47:1-2

I have to be honest, Ezekiel is a magnificent book but not altogether easy to fathom. However, the simple comparison I want to draw out of this picture is this: from the place where God resides (symbolised by the Temple) life-giving springs of water flow out bringing life to the world beyond. If you read on in Ezekiel 47 you will read of this happening. From God comes life-giving waters which spread out bringing life everywhere. If Eden is in some sense God's home on earth, His Temple we might call it, then it is perhaps not unsurprising that we are given a description of life-giving waters flowing out from God's presence that bring life to the world beyond. This idea is also found in Psalm 46:4 which says: There is a river whose streams make glad the city of God, the holy place where the Most High dwells.

To try and summarise, Eden was the focal point of God's presence on earth. Later, this presence became symbolised by his temple. And because God is the bringer of life, much as a river would have been in hot climates, we are given a picture of a river coming forth from Eden bringing life to the world beyond it, a world that mankind was to colonise and rule over. God, I suggest, is the one from whom flows living-giving water. Which leads me again to something Jesus said!

In John 4 we read a story about an encounter between Jesus and a Samaritan woman at Jacob's well. The disciples had left Jesus to have some 'me' space and gone off to the nearest town to buy provisions. As a Samaritan woman came to draw water at a time when she hoped to avoid hostility from others, she found herself being invited to draw water for Jesus to drink (she had no idea who he was at this stage). She found his request completely out of character with the customs of the day, as we read in John 4:9. But, as Jesus brilliantly draws her out and engages her, he says something incredibly profound:

> "Everyone who drinks this water will be thirsty again, but whoever drinks the water I give them will never thirst. Indeed the water I give them will become in them a spring of water, welling up to eternal life." John 4:13-14

Now, without going into too much detail, here was Jesus offering "living water" (John 4:10). Here was Jesus essentially comparing Himself to the spring coming forth from God's temple, the epicentre of God's presence. Jesus is claiming that *He* is now the one from whom will flow the waters of life. Again, as he tells his gospel account, John is supporting his incredible claim that Jesus was the fulfilment of the whole biblical account. He was the one who breathed life back into lifeless human beings; He was the one who could bring forth once more the life-giving waters from Eden.

But back to the first garden! The one water source is there described as separating into four: Genesis 2:10b. I mentioned earlier that numbers in Genesis are often very significant. Sevens are very important: they remind us of God's pattern in the creation and the setting apart of the seventh day as holy. Tens will also play their part. How clever that when God gave his people key commandments, these could more easily be remembered with reference to the ten digits they had on their hands (their fingers). As that seemed to be something of a struggle Jesus summarised this down to two: "'Love the Lord your God with all your heart, and with all your soul, and with all your mind.' This is the first and greatest commandment. And the second is like it" "Love your neighbour as yourself.'" (Matthew 22:37-38) (And, of course, we have two hands to remember them).

Threes abound too: they remind us of the God we know in three persons. But fours often seem to point to God's creation in its entirety: North, South, East and West. The four rivers named here, originating from the one, suggest that God's designs to bring life to the created world were not limited in any one direction but that He wished to see life spring forth across the whole world.

The names of the first two rivers are Pishon and the Gihon which are otherwise unknown to us. However, the name Havilah, the land through which the Pishon flows, is mentioned elsewhere in the Bible: Genesis 10:7, 29, 25:18, 1 Samuel 15:7, 1 Chronicles

1:9, 23. Commentators suggest that Havilah is found in Arabia. And Arabia was a source of gold in ancient times.[33] The additional note that 'aromatic resin and onyx are also there' v12, give the impression of wealth and beauty as is often identified with the splendour of God's presence and provision.

The second river, the Gihon, is described as winding its way through the whole land of Cush, v13. Cush usually refers to land of Ethiopia (Isaiah 20:3) although this is far from certain in this instance. Some commentators suggest that another Cush is meant, possibly located in Mesopotamia, which would make a connection with the location of the main headwater more plausible.[34]

The third and fourth rivers, the Tigris and the Euphrates, are still known to us. This mixture of names that are familiar and those that are unknown has led to many interesting theories about the potential location of Eden. There are certainly clues here but I'm not sure that is the thing the writer is especially interested in. Again, I fear, that this is typical of our predominantly literalistic desire to gain knowledge rather than seeking wisdom. *Wherever* Eden was, the picture given is of a beautiful paradise garden, flowing with life and abundance, rich in mineral wealth as well as a super-abundant food supply. A wonderful starting point for God's ultimate creation, human beings, to begin their mission. Which leads us to Genesis 2:15.

The LORD God took the man and put him in the Garden of Eden to work it and take care of it.   Genesis 2:15

33   Wenham, *Genesis 1-15*, p65
34   *Ibid*, p65-66

KNOWING OUR PLACE

This verse seems to pick up the thread from v8, as if verses 9 to 14 were something of an interlude from the main narrative. Verse 15 seems to outline the initial job description for the man made by God: he is to work the garden and take care of it.

Again, we need to remember that we are reading all these words as translations of the originals. The words we read as 'work it' could also be translated as to 'serve' or 'till' the ground. Whilst this is often how we would describe someone looking after the soil, it could also be used to describe someone 'serving God' or the duties of the Levites (the priestly tribe).[35] Similarly, Wenham notes that 'to take care of it' could also be translated 'to guard' or 'to keep'; these are also terms used to describe the religious duties of Levites to 'guard' the tabernacle of God (see Numbers 1:53, 3:7-8).[36] This connection suggests that part of the role of the man in caring for the Garden was to be understood as a religious duty. However, in calling it a *duty*, the text in no way suggests that this service was to be onerous. Far from it. Moreover, and contrary to the ideas of other ancient creation stories, this 'work' or 'service' was not oppressive or to be done for the benefit of God, but rather a delight to give the man true purpose and meaning. This is the sort of work of which he might say: I love what I do. (If you can say that of the work you do, I would say you - the reader - are greatly blessed!) So, just as God could stand back from the works of creation and say, it's good, I get the sense that Adam could similarly share the joy of

35 See Numbers 3:7-8
36 Wenham, *Genesis 1-15*, p67

his work well done and say: 'it is good'. But once more, just as we found there were limits to God's creative work, so the man is given one key restriction:

> And the LORD God commanded the man, "You are free to eat from any tree in the garden; but you must not eat from the tree of the knowledge of good and evil, for when you eat from it you will certainly die.
>
> Genesis 2:16-17

ANY TREE BAR ONE

We have observed already that when God made the man he did so intending to have a relationship with him. The man was so closely linked to God that he was made in God's image and likeness. Yet, despite that incredible proximity, the fact remained that God was God and the man was a creature created by God. They were not on a par. As such, it was perfectly reasonable for God to give the man an instruction. However, we can easily miss the fact that in this instruction we hear God's utter gracious generosity writ large: You are free to eat from *any* tree in the garden (italics added). *Any* tree! The man could enjoy each and every variety of fruit that the trees provided. His diet was vast and varied. God had given him so much to enjoy. All that was required of him was that he enjoy God's bounty and tend the garden.

However, there was a "but". As we noticed earlier, if their relationship was to be real, the man had to be offered the chance to make a choice other than the will of God. This is the "but". The man could eat from any tree, including therefore the tree of life, suggesting that Adam's full life was intended to be indefinite, but there was one limitation: but you must not eat from the tree of the knowledge of good and evil, for when you eat from it you will certainly die. There is no ambiguity here. God tells the man he must not eat from the tree of the knowledge of good and evil.

Since then, there has been intense debate and speculation about what this tree and its fruit represent.

> So, before I continue why not just pause a moment and ask yourself that same question: what do you think is meant by this tree and its placement here?

We might get some more clues as to what this tree represents as we continue the story, but for now we can draw out some initial thoughts:

Firstly, we need to remember, as we said before, that this was the *only* tree that God was denying the man access to. This was not the request of a tight and stingy God!

Secondly, the man *did* have access to the tree of life. There was no reason to take this forbidden fruit if God had commanded the man not to eat of it.

Thirdly, God placed the tree here so He did so for a good reason; remember, God had pronounced the whole creation as "very good".[37]

37 Genesis 1:31

Fourthly, there was no ambiguity to God's command: you must not eat from the tree of the knowledge of good and evil. This is as clear as God could be.

Fifthly, God set out a clear consequence in the man disobeying this command: you will certainly die.

Sixth, in the order of the narrative, this command is expressly given *just* to the man. The woman doesn't make an appearance till after this command is given.

And finally, now the man had the opportunity to do the very thing that God had told him not to do. But why would the man want to? To do so would be to do the very thing that God had expressly told him not to do. Whatever the man would have understood by 'dying', he knew enough to know that the good God who had given him life was telling him not to do it! Surely it was a no-brainer to simply obey! We might hope so.

THE KNOWLEDGE OF GOOD AND EVIL

Again, we need to pause here and consider afresh what is meant by the tree of the knowledge of good and evil. What is that knowledge? Taken literally, the tree seems to suggest the existence of two competing things: good and evil. They are polar extremes, diametrically opposite. And surely what is "good" would be worth knowing about, even if knowing evil wouldn't be. As I read this text it seems to me that the very instruction of God offers the means by which the man can determine which is which, something he wouldn't otherwise have known. In other words, you know the difference *when you disobey*. So, if the man should disobey the command of God and eat the forbidden fruit, in that instant he would discover something he didn't know before: that is what the difference between good and evil is. Prior to eating it, he did already know "good" since that was the pronouncement God had made over creation. But if he ate the fruit then he would become aware of the other extreme, what it means to do that which God commanded him not to do. It wasn't therefore anything about the fruit that would open his eyes to this knowledge, but the simple act of doing the thing that God had commanded him not to do! This therefore defines the difference very simply as follows: *good is that which God allows; evil is that which God forbids.* And the consequence of breaking God's command is that life, in some sense, will be forfeit. This makes sense because God is the giver of life. Therefore, to do as God commands is life-affirming. But to do anything that God calls us not to do is effectively to turn our backs on life, and that too is its polar opposite, which is of course 'death'.

So, in the very centre of God's paradise garden lay the choice of two paths: the man could continue to live in paradise as he had access to the tree of life. But he also had access to the means to choose self-autonomy. God allowed him that choice not to trick him, that isn't His nature, but to value him as a being truly made in his image. Two trees: two ways to live. What would he choose?

This leads me to another brief detour before we continue. This time looking at the close of Jesus' life on earth as told by Luke.

> Two other men, both criminals, were also led out with him to be executed. When they came to the place called the Skull, they crucified him there – one on his right, the other on his left.
>
> Luke 23:32-33

The Romans used crucifixion as a barbaric means to bring the life of a human being to an end. It was a punishment designed to make that end as painful and terrible as could be imagined. It told the world in no uncertain terms that Rome was in charge and if anyone should be so foolish as to disobey Rome they'd pay for it in the most extreme way. Men were literally nailed to a wooden cross and left there to die. And, as Luke describes the moment when Jesus was led out to suffer this unjust death, two other guilty men (criminals) were led out to be crucified with him. They would be nailed to two wooden crosses (there is again the imagery of two trees) with Jesus nailed to a third between them.

Luke continues:

> There was a written notice above him (Jesus), which read: THIS IS THE KING OF THE JEWS. One of the criminals who hung there hurled insults at him: "Aren't you the Messiah? Save yourself and us!" But the other criminal rebuked him. "Don't you fear God," he said, "since you are under the under the same sentence? We are punished justly, for we are getting what our deeds deserve. But this man has done nothing wrong." Then he said, "Jesus, remember me when you come into your kingdom." Jesus answered him, "Truly I tell you, today you will be with me in paradise."
>
> Luke 23:38-43

Did you hear the subtle reminder of the two trees of Eden in this story? Both men knew the difference between good and evil and they realised that their punishment was justified. They had made their choices, apparently choosing to do that which was evil rather than that which was good, and death was to be their reward. But the second man, as he hung in agony, made a different choice: he turned instead to the tree of life! You will remember that the tree of life is often equated with wisdom in the Bible. You might also remember that the fear of the LORD is the beginning of wisdom.[38] So this man spoke with true wisdom when he asked his fellow criminal: "Don't you fear God?" The implication here of course is that he *did* fear God. And, as he watched Jesus hanging on the cross next to him, he recognized in Jesus the true image of God in a man "who had done nothing wrong". This second man, knowing that he faced death, feared God and put his faith in Jesus; he chose to put his trust in God again by believing in Jesus. And what an amazing promise Jesus gave him for so doing:

"Truly I tell you, today you will be with me in paradise." Jesus effectively promised the man that, because of his faith in him, when he died (the result of knowing good and evil) he would go beyond death back to the garden paradise where he would be with God once more!

This is about as incredible as it gets! Even though our Genesis account warns us that the consequence of choosing the knowledge of good and evil will result in death, the work of Jesus dying on the cross shows us that there is a way back, a way beyond death, a way for a guilty man to be restored to paradise. The key to this is the wisdom that fears the LORD and puts its trust

38 Proverbs 1:7

in wisdom personified, Jesus: the one who did nothing wrong, who always did as the Father commanded, who died in our place and offers us a way back to paradise. It doesn't get any better than that!!

GOD'S CROWNING GLORY

Having set this final piece of the plan in place, now we get to meet God's final created being, his crowning glory!

> The LORD God said, "It is not good for the man to be alone. I will make a helper suitable for him." Genesis 2:18

For the very first time in the creation story we come across something that God describes as being "not good". And that is that the man is 'alone'. Bilezikian says of this verse that "God's supreme achievement was not the creation of solitary man, but the creation of human community."[39] Thus the situation that is not good is the man being alone. God's remedy to this aloneness is to make a helper suitable for him. The woman is to be a rescuer for this state of affairs. That, suggests Bilezikian, is the true meaning of 'suitable helper'.[40] The only reason given in the text for the creation of the woman was to stop the man being alone.

Now some have taken the idea of the woman being a 'helper' to denote some degree of inferiority or subservience. But biblically this is untenable. Elsewhere the use of the word 'helper'

39 G. Bilezikian, *Community 101*, Grand Rapids, Michigan: Zondervan, 1997, p19
40 Bilezikian, *Community*, p20

is used of God providing the help.[41] To help someone does not imply that the helper is either stronger or weaker than the one helped, only that the one offers assistance to the other for a need they may be unable to resolve alone, as is the case here. The writer doesn't proceed to explain straight away how it is that the helper will be given but seems to delight in building the suspense.

So next we read:

> Now the LORD God had formed out of the ground all the wild animals and all the birds in the sky. He brought them to the man to see what he would name them; and whatever the man called each living creature, that was its name. So the man gave names to all the livestock, the birds in the sky and all the wild animals. But for Adam no suitable helper was found.
>
> Genesis 2:19-20

Recapping on some of the details of creation which we observed in Genesis 1, we are reminded that God formed the animals and birds from the ground: physical beings made from the same essential building block as the man yet lacking that distinctive quality of being made in the image and likeness of God. Further, as if to solidify the sense that the man is to have dominion over all the other creatures, God delegates the role of giving each a name to the man.[42] We're told that God brought the animals and birds to the man to be named, but the suggestion of v20 is that they were also being put on show to see if there was any

---

41 For example: Hosea 13:9
42 In the Ancient Near East, when a ruler named people or things it was considered to be an act of claiming dominion of them.

creature that could solve the problem of Adam's 'aloneness'.[43] If the man was to truly experience community on anything like a par with that known by God, then only a being who was of the same essence as him would suffice. And despite the parade of the animals and birds no suitable helper was identified.

The "so" that introduces the verses that follow are God's remedy for this "not good" situation and serve as God's finale in the creation process.

> So the LORD caused the man to fall into a deep sleep; and while he was sleeping, he took one of the man's ribs and then closed up the place with flesh. Then the LORD God made a woman from the rib he had taken out of the man, and he brought her to the man.
>
> Genesis 2:21-22

Now I'm sure that if you have been around churches for long enough you will have heard these verses discussed and commented on. For a start, having discounted all the other creations as not adequate to deal with the man's aloneness, it was therefore incumbent upon God to step in to solve the problem. Indeed, that point is worth taking particular note of. The man, then in a state of aloneness, could not resolve his own situation. He could not create "community" for himself. The man's problem could not have been fixed with any amount of knowledge gained from the tree of the knowledge of good and evil. He had life but he couldn't know 'one-ness in love' with one of the same 'being' merely as he was; love is *always* other-centred and there

---

43 Suggestions that the dog came highly commended as a possibility cannot be substantiated.

was no 'other' to be centred on. Without his 'helper', the man could never experience the love that God knew within Himself by virtue of being three persons in an interdependent bond of community. His 'helper' would enable the man to truly image God in a way that he couldn't without her. But unless God stepped in to make her, the man was stuck 'alone'. One might say that without God's help the man could not be 'saved' from his situation. Salvation needed to come from outside himself, and since none of the other creations could fix it, then the only means of salvation had to come from God.

A DEEP SLEEP

Now, again at this point, I want to interject another brief detour. We read that God caused the man to fall into a deep sleep. God needed to do this to begin his work of dealing with the man's essential problem, his aloneness. Some time ago, a friend of mine preached on a parallel to this idea that God put the man into a deep sleep.[44] My attention was drawn to the way that Jesus often referred to those who had died as if they had fallen asleep.[45] When eventually, Jesus also died and was placed in a tomb, he too entered his own 'deep sleep' as had his friend Lazarus after *he* died. We might say that God put Jesus into a deep sleep, until such time as he raised him from death on the third day.

After Genesis 3 (and we'll get to that in a moment) the Bible speaks about all humans having a basic problem. We too are 'alone' in

44 Unpublished sermon by Pastor Andy Woof at Garstang Free Methodist church.
45 John 11:11

the sense that we are no longer connected to our life source: God. In that way we, the collective human race, could be described as being 'alone' as we find ourselves now living separate from God. And, in that state, despite all our acquired knowledge, we have not been able to overcome our essential inheritance from that loss of relationship. We all face death. But, and this is the biggest 'but' that history has ever known, God, having allowed Jesus to be crucified for our sakes to bear in himself the separation that belongs to us all, placed Jesus into the deep sleep of death. But, on that first Easter Sunday, the Spirit of God woke him from that death and gave him new life![46] Just as the woman is the new start that solved the first man's problem, so the resurrection of Jesus, following his crucifixion and death on our behalf, is the new start that says to us all that our separation from God is no more!

To further substantiate this parallel, we might also consider the place that God operated on the man to bring forth his new life: his rib. You may well have heard speakers suggesting that God took a rib, close to the man's heart rather than part of the man's head or feet so that she would be at his side rather than be over him or under him. Make of those ideas what you may. But the point I wish to draw out is the parallel again to the death of Jesus. In John 19:31-34 we read:

> 'Now it was the day of Preparation, and the next day was to be a special Sabbath. Because the Jewish leaders did not want the bodies to be left on the crosses during the Sabbath, they asked Pilate to have the legs broken and the bodies taken down'.[47] 'The soldiers therefore came and broke the legs of

46 Romans 8:11
47 By breaking their legs, those being crucified could no longer push themselves up on their crosses and keep breathing and so would die sooner.

the first man who been crucified with Jesus, and then those of the other. But when they came to Jesus and found that he was already dead, they did not break his legs. Instead, one of the soldiers *pierced Jesus' side* with a spear bringing a sudden flow of blood and water'. (Italics added)

Just as God took a rib from the first man's side to bring new life in the woman, which would lead to the resolution of the aloneness of the man being resolved, so the Roman soldier pierced the side of Jesus to confirm his death, the death which enabled new life to come to us all. This provided the resolution to humanity's ultimate problem of aloneness, our separation from God.[48]

I have to mention too that, just as God brought the woman to the man when he awoke from his deep sleep (Genesis 2:22), do you remember who it was that first witnessed the risen Christ when he rose from his? We briefly mentioned her story earlier. When Jesus was raised from his 'deep sleep' of death, the first encounter he had was also with a woman, with Mary Magdalene.[49] This Mary didn't come from His side, but she was brought to spiritual life through her faith in Jesus and truly gave herself to him as a disciple.

When the first man, who we don't yet have a name for, was introduced to the woman, I love his exclamation of joy (well that's how I read it anyway):[50]

48 2 Corinthians 5:15 says: 'And he died for all, that those who live should no longer live for themselves but for him who died for them and was raised again.'
49 John 20:11-18
50 Wenham reads it this way too: Wenham, *Genesis 1-15*, p.70

"This is now bone of my bones and flesh of my flesh;
She shall be called 'woman,' for she was taken out of man."

Genesis 2:23

SHE SHALL BE CALLED 'WOMAN'

Again, we miss the brilliance of this compact poetry in our English translations, but commentators suggest this statement employs numerous Hebrew poetic techniques to emphasize the man's wonder at this new creation.[51]

What this declaration does is to state clearly that the man and the woman are to be on an equal footing as each other with regard to their humanity and yet set apart from all the other animals.

Now much has been made of the man calling her 'woman' in this poem. As we saw earlier, the process of someone giving a name to another was understood in the Ancient Near East as claiming dominion over the one so named. Thus, it has sometimes been suggested, the woman is in some sense to be subordinate to the man. Many commentators certainly read it this way.[52] However, before the man gave the woman this title, we find that it has already been given to her by God: Verse 22 reads:

'Then the LORD God made a woman from the rib he had taken out of the man, and he brought her to the man.' This also differs from the process we read earlier in the chapter when we noted:

51 *Ibid* p70
52 *Ibid* p70

He (God) brought them (the animals) to the man to see what he would name them Genesis 2:19. There is no sense that God brought the woman to the man to be named for it appears that he had already given her that name 'woman,' as we read in verse 22. Indeed, it isn't until Genesis 3:20 that we find Adam giving his wife a name; but we'll ask ourselves more about that when we get there.

So, there is perhaps good cause to see here no sense of hierarchy or dominion in the man's ecstatic outburst of delight: her being named as a 'woman' by the man is simply a repetition of that name which God has already used of her. God really did have dominion over the woman, just as he did over the man, since *he* created them both.[53]

With the introduction of the woman, the man's aloneness is a conquered foe and now the commandment of God to "Be fruitful and increase in number" Genesis 1:28 can be realised.

BECOMING ONE AGAIN

As we come to verse 24, this doesn't seem to continue the man's statement but reads as a summary statement inserted into the text to draw an important conclusion. The verse should probably begin with the word "Therefore" but in the NIV it reads:

> That is why a man leaves his father and mother and is united to his wife, and they become one flesh.   Genesis 2:24

53 Bilezikian, *Community 101*, p21

Once more, this simple verse has major implications for how human beings are to organise themselves and what God's good plans for them were.[54] If we begin by recapping just for a moment, we have just read how the woman was literally taken out of the man. His problem of aloneness is now resolved as the man and woman can now live as community together. As part of the man (his rib) was taken to make the woman, so he is now only 'complete' when they are reunited as one. And just as the woman was taken out of the man, so every future human being whether male or female shall come forth from a woman. I love the sense of interdependence that God has thus established here between the sexes. The pattern for the outworking of the man/ woman union is now established. The man and woman were the initial pairing: they were to be 'father and mother'. But their union, we're not given the details, will result in the fulfilment of God's instruction to be fruitful and increase in number. When they come together as man and woman in a sexual union, they will be able to produce a new life. (We can see something of the sheer wonder and extraordinary nature of this, so well expressed in Louie Giglio's 'How Great is Our God video').[55]

We can so easily take the incredible nature of this for granted, can't we? We just accept it as part of the fabric of life. But the whole process of the formation of a new human life is a profound mystery. I love how the Psalmist puts it in Psalm 139:

54 Wenham says of this verse: 'This account of woman's origin explains the experience of every couple that in marriage they become related to each other as though they were blood relatives: "they become one flesh." Indeed, the marriage bond is even stronger than that between parent and child, for "a man forsakes his father and mother and sticks to his wife," an astounding declaration in a world where filial duty was the most sacred obligation next to loyalty to God.' Wenham, *Genesis 1-15*, p87-88
55 https://www.youtube.com/watch?v=atUGBua2AzE

For you created my inmost being; you knit me together in my mother's womb.
I praise you because I am fearfully and wonderfully made; your works are wonderful,
I know that full well.
My frame was not hidden from you when I was made in the secret place, when I was woven together in the depths of the earth.
Your eyes saw my unformed body; all the days ordained for me were written in your book before one of them came to be.   Psalm 139:13-16

Those verses alone could form the foundation of a study in their own right, but suffice to say, in our original human father and mother lay the potential for each and every human life that was to come. And the creation of each and every subsequent new life is known to God. As we used to say in our church: "Every life matters to God" and "All your life matters to God".

However, this verse has something else to teach us about how this new human community should function. When a man was at an age where he was old enough to come out from the covering/protection of his father and mother (we're not given details here about when this would be but simply told that it would happen), then he would also follow in the way of his first father and be united to his own wife. They would thus form a new nuclear family of a man and woman and would then continue that process of becoming one flesh (and hence continuing the process of being fruitful as God instructed). There is absolutely no sense here that any such union would be a temporary arrangement; far from it. The leaving of father and mother is to be superseded by a permanent union with his own wife. This is God's ordained pattern for the formation of human society: a man leaving his father and mother and being united to his own wife and them sharing an inseparable union of oneness; this would then produce the wonder of the creation of new human life. This was God's best plan: pure and simple.

NAKED AND UNASHAMED

So, we have now almost completed all that is necessary in our prologue to set the course of God's story going. Everything is in place. We're not told again that this was "good", but the concluding verse of Genesis 2 sets the seal on these opening chapters in much the same way:

> Adam and his wife were both naked, and they felt no shame.
>
> Genesis 2:25

If we didn't notice before, the man is here referred to by the name 'Adam' (as he was in verse 20) which essentially means 'the man'. Woman means something like 'taken out of the man' as verse 23 suggests. She will receive a personal name in the next chapter. But the chapter concludes with the first human pair, the man and his wife, both naked and unashamed. As well as serving as a fitting end to the story of how God's creative work was brought to its fitting climax, it also links with what will transpire as we move into the next phase of the story, which we know as Genesis 3.

But why do we need this detail? Wenham notes that the Hebrew root 'to be ashamed' does not carry the overtones of personal guilt that English 'shame' includes. Hebrew can speak of 'shame' triggered by circumstances completely extrinsic to the speaker. He cites Judges 3:25 and 2 Kings 2:17 as examples.[56] So, an alternative understanding might be that the couple really weren't concerned about their nudity; just like any very young child. The picture here is of complete purity. There is no guilt, no shame, no embarrassment at any level, no sense of anything other than delight in each other and the home that God had created for them. One might even say of their existence that there was no death, no mourning, no crying or pain.[57] Rather Adam and his wife knew only life in all its fulness.[58] And with access to the tree of life (Genesis 2:9) there was no reason for this situation to change. However, the story goes on....

56 Wenham, *Genesis 1-15*, p71.
57 See Revelation 21:4
58 See John 10:10

3.
GENESIS 3
The Villain

INTRODUCING THE VILLAIN

Nearly every story has a villain and we're about to be introduced
to the villain of the Bible story.

> Now the serpent was more crafty than any of the wild animals the LORD God
> had made.
>
> Genesis 3:1.

Having finished the previous section (Chapter 2) on such a high,
the entry of the serpent is quite jarring. Immediately his description as "more crafty" alerts the reader to the potential danger that
is associated with him. Crafty, as the NIV has it, could similarly
be translated as "shrewd" or even "prudent'. It is a somewhat

ambiguous term because when it is used in Proverbs 12:16 or
13:16 it is something the wise person should pursue. However, it is
also used in other situations where it has negative connotations.[59]
The use of this word actually links in with the end of chapter 2
very cleverly. This is another one of those situations where the
Hebrew play on words is virtually lost in the English translation.
It works a little better if we tweak the words and compare the
man and his wife who have just been described as being "nude"
encountering the serpent who is described as being "shrewd".

The reality is though, that we are also told that the serpent is
one of the wild animals the LORD God had made. This raises
a multitude of obvious questions.

> You might like to pause at this point and record some
> of your own, though I am not promising that we'll find
> easy answers.

Again, a clue to explaining this strange scene may be found in
other ancient creation sources, the Gilgamesh Epic in particular.[60]
In that story, Gilgamesh found a plant through which he could
avoid death. Unfortunately, while he was swimming in a pond,
a snake came out and swallowed the plant, thereby depriving
him of the chance of immortality.[61] The connections to our story
are clear but there are significant differences.[62]

59 Job 5:12: 'He thwarts the plans of the crafty, so that their hands achieve no
    success.'
60 According to Wikipedia the Gilgamesh Epic is an epic poem from ancient
    Mesopotamia, regarded as the earliest surviving notable literature and the
    second oldest religious text, after the Pyramid Texts.
61 Wenham, Genesis 1-15, p72
62 As Wenham notes, whilst the Gilgamesh Epic and the Genesis account both
    involve a snake, man, plants, and the promise of life, in the Genesis account

Another thing we might note is that later in Israelite history, animals were categorised as being either clean or unclean (See Leviticus 11). In view of its means of movement, a snake or serpent would be categorised as being as unclean as any animal could be. Within the world of the Old Testament animal symbolism, a snake would therefore be an ideal candidate for an anti-God symbol - even if it was originally created by God. So, as Wenham notes: 'For an Israelite familiar with the symbolic values of different animals, a creature more likely than a serpent to lead man away from his creator could not be imagined'.[63]

As the Bible story progresses we may find additional clues as to the origin and nature of this character but, for now, we have certainly been given notice that he needs to be given very careful attention, especially when we hear his first utterance, and especially when we observe who he said it to!

He (the serpent) said to the woman, "Did God really say, 'You must not eat from any tree in the garden'?"
Genesis 3:1

DID GOD REALLY SAY?

The first thing to note is the obvious question of how it was that a snake was able to converse with humans? We might remember what we said about the different genres found in a daily newspaper and how cartoons involving talking animals (such as Fred Bassett or Snoopy) are simply accepted by the reader who rec-

the man loses his immortality through blatant disobedience, in the epic that loss seems to be just a matter of bad luck. Wenham, *Genesis 1-15*, p73
63 *Ibid* p73

ognises this genre for what it is and understands that points of truth can be made in this way. For the genre of literature here, questions of talking animals don't seem to be that important.

Secondly, we might note that, just as God addressed the man in Genesis 2:16-17, here the serpent addresses the woman who *wasn't present* when God's instructions were originally given. Immediately we are reminded of the insidious technique of 'divide and conquer' as we begin to see the serpent's craftiness playing out. By engaging the secondary source, the woman, rather than the primary source, the man who directly received God's instructions, there is likely to be more room for doubt. It also serves to begin to undermine God's order in things, but more of that later.

We might also note the subtle way that the serpent refers to God in this verse. Previously God is described as "The LORD God."[64] However when the serpent refers to him, he describes him only as 'God': "Did God really say...". The serpent thus already shows a lack of personal connectedness and lack of submission to his maker. We might note here that he is thus showing himself to be the opposite of wise (remember: 'the fear of the LORD is the beginning of wisdom' Proverbs 1:7) even if he is described as 'crafty'. This character is already portrayed as one who is the personification of a rebellious spirit and someone who seems to believe independence from God is a more appealing scenario than living with God as LORD. Thus, his initial question to the woman may not come as a complete

---

64 **LORD** usually translates Yahweh (Jehovah), the sacred covenant name of **God**. God usually translates elohim, which appears to **mean** something like «the mighty one.»

surprise: "Did God really say, 'You must not eat from any tree in the garden'?"

By phrasing the question as he does, there is immediately a belittling of, and distancing from, God (not referring to him as "The LORD God") as we observed, as well as a complete reversal of God's generous provision. If we revisit what God actually said to the man we read: "You are free to eat from *any* tree in the garden" (Genesis 2:16): the *only* restriction God gave was that the man "must not eat from the tree of the knowledge of good and evil". In the way that the serpent phrased his question, God's generosity is made to sound like a gross unfairness as if God was holding back something good. The phasing is already so subtle and so insidious, and one wonders how the first human couple, so free in the innocence of their nakedness, will be able to hold out against such a corrupted and scheming foe. It feels like the challenge has begun and we watch with interest, and no little concern, to see how the woman will respond.

> The woman said to the serpent, "We may eat fruit from the trees in the garden, but God did say, 'You must not eat fruit from the tree that is in the middle of the garden, and you must not touch it, or you will die.'"
>
> Genesis 3:2-3.

DON'T TOUCH?

What the woman *should* have said to the serpent at this point would have been something like: 'We may eat from *every* tree in the garden, but the *LORD* God told us not to eat from just one tree because the consequences of doing so would be terrible for us.' But the reply the woman gave wasn't this and straight away we see that the craftiness of the serpent is poisoning her mind. Instead of acknowledging God's gracious and generous provision, that they could eat from 'every tree', she has been deceived into thinking that God was less than generous. Furthermore, instead of calling him 'the LORD God', the woman refers to God in the same way that the serpent had, just as 'God'. However, note the addition of an extra dimension to God's commandment not to eat from the tree in the middle of the garden: they 'must not touch it"! This is something God had *not* said to the man and shows that she is being deceived into siding with the serpent.

Now, in this simple communication we learn so much about the tactics of this wily serpent:

He seeks to undermine the human's confidence in the goodness of God.

He seeks to make them underestimate the generosity of God and, instead, see any restrictions God makes as an unnecessary limitation to their freedom and potential fulfilment.

Furthermore, he doesn't discourage them from becoming more legalistic in their understanding of God than is truly the case (you must not touch it).

In all this we can see clearly that the seed of doubt, once sown, can easily lead to a full-blown rejection of their once-blissful relationship with God and their surroundings. Instead, what was once paradise can start to appear as a something restrictive and stifling. Such is the devastating power unleashed by the serpent. Now, having drawn her this far, the serpent's next statement is a *direct challenge* to the authority of God:

> "You will not certainly die," the serpent said to the woman. "For God knows that when you eat from it your eyes will be opened, and you will be like God, knowing good and evil."
>
> Genesis 3:4-5

YOUR EYES WILL BE OPENED

The subtlety and cleverness of this reply confirm afresh the description of the serpent as 'crafty'. It's really powerful to the story that the woman, having been drawn into the serpent's trap of half-truths and insinuation, has exaggerated the restriction spoken by God to the man. In Genesis 2:17 God had told him not to eat from the tree of knowledge of good and evil. To which, led on by the serpent's insinuation that God wasn't so generous as she thought, the woman had added that they "must not touch it or you will die." The serpent's reply: "You will not certainly die," is probably true. God hadn't told Adam he'd die if he touched the forbidden fruit. But this leads the serpent to suggest that, rather than dying, if they ate the fruit 'their eyes would be opened and they would be like God, knowing good and evil.' In one sense, this was indeed true as we'll see.

But the absolute tragedy of this encounter was that God's motives were called into question without any consideration or evaluation of those of the serpent. What was he trying to achieve in this exchange? The serpent's whole approach of undermining the woman's confidence in the goodness and trustworthiness of God served to have her effectively placing her trust in the serpent's deceit. What was happening here was that her allegiance was shifting from the God who had given her life, to a creature made by God; one over whom God had made the human pair to have dominion (Genesis 1:28). Instead of the true order of things God > humans (man and woman) > animals, the serpent had effectively placed himself at the head of the chain. With this terrible poison now discharged, we look with alarm to see what effect this will have on the woman.

> When the woman saw that the fruit of the tree was good for food and pleasing to the eye, and also desirable for gaining wisdom, she took some and ate it. She also gave some to her husband who was with her, and he ate it. Genesis 3:6

AND THEY ATE

This is possibly the most tragic verse in the Bible. If you remember the way that Genesis 2:5-3:24 is carefully structured into seven scenes, when we come to verses 3:6-8, we arrive at the crucial central scene: this is the most significant moment in the narrative. The key aspects of Genesis 3:6 can be summarised very simply as: She saw, she took, she ate and she gave. And in this brief but clever description we learn so much about the power of seduction to turn a human being away from God.

To begin with, the serpent isn't mentioned in this scene. His poison sown, he can stand back and watch as it takes effect without any direct culpability. The woman is now positioned at the middle of the garden (Genesis 2:9) where the trees of life and the knowledge of good and evil were placed. With all the other trees freely available, all incidentally described already as good for food and pleasing to the eye (see Genesis 2:9), to put herself so close to temptation was a major risk. But not only was she *there* but she is described as *gazing* at the fruit; the woman saw that the fruit of the tree was good for food and pleasing to the eye.

The more we allow ourselves to focus on that which we know we shouldn't, the more our resolve will diminish and we will be drawn into doing that which we know to be wrong. It would be just as if an alcoholic were to sit outside a public house: how much that would drastically reduce his/her capacity to resist going in for a drink. They would be far wiser to keep far away. There are times and situations where our only safety is in staying away from danger. Sadly, the woman was drawn towards it and didn't resist. As she looked at the fruit it became more and more enticing. Not only did it offer the potential of being good for food (not that she needed that with the multitude of other fruits freely available) but it was pleasing to the eye.

How clever this expression is in summing up how temptation operates. We begin to doubt that that which we know to be wrong, and potentially dangerous, really is. We doubt the goodness of God and think we know better. We get drawn in to being close to the object of temptation. And, as we look too long at that which we know we shouldn't, whether it be eating a forbidden fruit or whatever the temptation might be, the more it takes on a kind of supernatural attraction. We find ourselves almost under its spell and unable to perceive the danger anymore. And, if we linger too long, we can convince ourselves that what we know to be wrong is even something that will be good for us: here described as desirable for gaining wisdom.

Now, of course, we know this can't be true. As we've noted several times, wisdom begins with the fear of the LORD. In this instance, the taking of the fruit, expressly forbidden by God, cannot be a means of gaining wisdom since it involves *not* fearing the LORD. The serpent had promised that by eating the fruit she would be like God, knowing good and evil. The irony of course is that when God made the man and the woman they were *already* 'like' him; they were expressly described as being made in his image and likeness (Genesis 1:26-27). What they weren't aware of was the knowledge of 'evil', which we described previously as doing that which God had commanded them not to do. That awareness could only come from this direct action. Again, the serpent's clever use of half-truths and direct challenges to the guidance of God play out in the woman's actions. So we arrive at the tragic consequence of all this: she took some and she ate it. The line had been crossed. The woman had effectively transferred her allegiance from God to the serpent in this one simple action; she took and she ate. And then, typically of what happens when we do that which we know we shouldn't, the woman also 'gave some to her husband, who was with her, and he ate it. When we do what we know we shouldn't, we might feel better about it if we can point to another and say, they did it too!

It's one thing that the woman was deceived but what was Adam thinking? He'd received the *direct* instruction from God (Genesis 2:17). He knew that God had told him not to eat of the forbidden fruit. Why hadn't he spoken up? What was he doing in this danger zone? And what on earth was he doing joining his wife in eating this expressly forbidden fruit? *If* Adam did have any element of authority over his wife, as some suggest, then why wasn't he exercising that authority? Whether that authority was real or otherwise, Adam is not recorded as saying anything. He simply goes along with his wife's, God rejecting, action. So, they took, and they ate, and the result of so doing would all too soon become evident.

> "She *took* some and *ate* it. She also gave some to her husband, who was with her, and he ate it."
>
> Genesis 3:6

That was the moment, the terrible moment when all the beauty and wonder of creation was undone. The whole wondrous creation, made by God for his incredible beloved humans to enjoy and share with him, was undone in a bite. She took and ate, and so did he, and God's dream was shattered.

In a much smaller way but a similar dynamic, it's a little like the moment I tell my dog to stand still; she hears my voice and yet turns away and heads in the opposite direction. Self-will wins out and the bond of love is cut. The action effectively says: I know best and I'll do as I please. My will not yours be done. So Adam and Eve were deceived into an action that saw the serpent heard rather than God. Our authority became his and our spiritual oneness with God died.

TAKE AND EAT

But before we go on to unpack the dreadful damage that this tragic revolt against God would unleash, I want to quickly pause and consider the way in which this terrible incident would eventually be turned on its head!

After this incident their close relationship with their maker was lost and the human pair would no longer be allowed to remain in God's garden paradise. We are left with questions wondering how God could persuade humans that they were wrong to mistrust him? And how could God make good this damage? What they did in 'taking' what was forbidden would one day be completely turned on its head; but it would take God himself to make good this terrible misjudgement! So how would God ever bring us back from this?

This is the wonder of the Easter story! And here is a sneak peep forward in the story to get a glimpse of how he'd do so.

Skip forward to Luke 22:14. As Jesus sat with his friends, his disciples, at that Passover supper in the upper room, this is what Jesus said:

> When the hour came, Jesus and his apostles reclined at the table. And he said to them, "I have eagerly desired to eat this Passover with you before I suffer. For I tell you, I will not eat it again until it finds fulfilment in the kingdom of God." After taking the cup, he gave thanks and said, "Take this and divide it among you. For I tell you I will not drink again from the fruit of the vine until the kingdom of God comes." And he took bread, gave thanks and broke it, and

gave it to them, saying, "This is my body given for you; do this in remembrance of me." In the same way, after the supper he took the cup, saying, "This cup is the new covenant in my blood, which is poured out for you.

Luke 22:14-20

At that Passover meal, when the Jews celebrated that first Passover event, the whole point was that they remembered. They remembered that they had been slaves in Egypt. They had become human-doings, not human-beings; fit only to be the slave labour force of Egypt. But they had cried out to God for liberation from their cruel oppressors and God had sent them a rescuer.

Since that moment in the garden, all humanity has been slaves too; slaves to sin.

At that first Passover, after God had sent 9 plagues to unmask the false gods of Egypt and to show the Pharaoh who was really in charge, still the Pharaoh refused to let God's people go. So Moses, God's rescuer, warned him that one final plague would come. The angel of death would be unleashed over Egypt and the first born of every family would die. And that would apply to the Israelites too. But God gave them a way that the plague of death would 'pass-over' their homes. They were to prepare a meal: they were to take a lamb without defect and kill it and its blood was to be smeared on the doorposts and lintel of their homes. Once its life-blood had been poured out and used to cover their homes they took and ate its flesh. Thus, when the angel of death came, any home that was covered and thus protected by the lamb's blood, would be passed over. The animal's death became their substitute and they were spared. Only then, with Egypt unprotected and reeling with grief at their losses, did the Pharaoh let the Israelites go to find freedom. And that Passover meal became an annual reminder to the Israelites that God had saved them and redeemed them by the blood of the lamb.

Fast forward to that upper room and here was Jesus, described already in John 1:29 as the Lamb of God who takes away the sin of the world, sharing that same Passover feast with his friends. Only this time, as Jesus took bread, he gave thanks and broke it: then he gave it to them saying, 'This is my body given for you; do this in remembrance of me" Luke 22:19. In other words Jesus said to his disciples: Take, eat!

Here, in this incredibly well-known passage, we hear Jesus calling those who had followed him for the three years of his earthly ministry to 'take' something into themselves. Did you hear the echo?

> After *taking* the cup, he gave thanks and said, "*Take* this and divide it among you."
> And he *took* bread, gave thanks and broke it, and gave it to them, saying, "This is my body given for you; do this in remembrance of me."
> After the supper he *took* the cup, saying, "This cup is the new covenant in my blood, which is poured out for you.

Just as the serpent persuaded the first humans to *take* the forbidden fruit into themselves so, as Jesus prepared to go to the cross, He asked His followers to *take* fruit once more. This time it was the fruit of the vine which represented *His* blood to be poured out for them. And the fruit of the earth, the bread, that represented *His* body broken for them.

Adam and his wife *took* that which was off-limits to them and it brought about their death (we'll consider that in just a moment). Jesus asked his followers to *take* that which He provided, representing the fruit of His life given over for them, and promised them life!

Thus, in the same manner that these first humans failed, essentially by not trusting God, Jesus succeeded by trusting God, even at the cost of his own life. And by so doing he 'took' back the authority that the serpent had so craftily taken from the humans and began the work of reordering creation.

In the garden there was a fruit God had told the human pair not to eat. They ate and paradise was lost to them. Now, in that upper room, Jesus took bread, and gave it to them saying: Take, eat! This is my body broken for you. **In so doing God made the greatest reversal the world has ever known:**

The first human pair took and ate what brought them death. Now Jesus *took* their death into himself, and invited *them* to take life into themselves and eat the fruit of life.

> And after supper he took the cup saying, "This cup is the new covenant in my blood, which is poured out for you"
>
> Luke 22:20

BLOOD POURED OUT FOR YOU

Back in the garden, when the first human pair ate of the forbidden fruit their eyes were opened and they realised they were naked, they hid from each other and from God. They hid their nakedness with fig leaves. But when God came looking for them, He graciously replaced their flimsy coverings with skin; animal skin. There, in the garden, the first recorded death in the Bible seems to have been that of an animal who died so that the human's guilt and shame might be covered. The animal's life blood was given that they might be able to live on. Its skin covered their nakedness.

When Jesus had shared the Passover meal with his disciples He said to them 'after supper', that is after they had eaten, that the cup of wine represented His blood which was about to be poured out for them. In other words, like that first sacrificial animal whose death covered them, now that they had eaten, his sacrifice was to be made to set them free. But this was not from slavery to Egypt but a far greater enemy, sin itself! This was Jesus saying that His blood was the blood to be taken into themselves so that the angel of death would pass over them once more.

This was the moment that Jesus showed them God's new promise. Just as all humanity were condemned to die in Adam, so all humanity were now offered life in Christ. His blood, His death would count for them. But this was no longer an external thing, no more covering doorposts and lintels, now the blood (wine in this case that stood for the blood) would be taken inwards, taken into themselves. Christ would bring about an inward change.

Take EAT became not just the cause of the problem but it's very remedy: the sacrifice of the lamb would once more cover their sin and set them free!

Now, every time you *take* into yourself the bread and cup of the Lord's Supper, the Eucharist, or whatever term you choose to employ, you are celebrating the reversal that Jesus brought of this tragic defeat. Every cup of wine/juice, every wafer of bread you take into yourself reverses that first fruit that the man and his wife took into themselves. The action that brought death is used by Jesus to bring back life!

But all that is to jump well ahead in our story. For now, what we have is the dreadful moment that the first human couple did the very thing, the only thing, that God had told them not to do. So what was the result?

To summarise what we've said, the woman here 'took' the fruit that she and her husband had been told not to eat. It was their taking the fruit in to themselves, and in so doing the rejection of God, that God told Adam would lead to death. We'll unpack that 'death' in a moment. But essentially what this story highlights is that the first human couple doubted God's goodness toward them, believed a lie about Him, and did the very thing, indeed the only thing, He told them not to do.

EYES WIDE OPEN

Then the eyes of both of them were opened, and they realised they were naked; so they sewed fig leaves together and made coverings for themselves.

Genesis 3:7.

The way this whole episode is carefully structured and set out in the text is deliberately designed to make "and he ate" the turning point of the episode. Before this moment the woman had such hopes for what would happen if she, and indeed her husband, ate the forbidden fruit. She describes it as: "good for food", "pleasing to the eye" and "desirable for gaining wisdom". But after they ate these expressions are balanced out by what happened afterwards: "the eyes of both of them were opened", "they realised they were naked" and shortly we will read of them hiding from the LORD God.

The serpent had led the woman to believe that by doing this one thing, the very thing the LORD God had told them not to do, they would receive so much more than they had. What actually transpired was that they lost so much of what they already did have. They did gain the knowledge that they didn't previously have of the difference between good and evil. That was true. But it didn't give the benefits the woman may have expected. Instead, they now knew what it meant to do the one thing God had commanded them not to do and it had cost them their innocence, their connectedness with each other and, worse, their connection with God. Now, instead of the beautiful freedom of their nakedness, they were only able to hide their shame with a ridiculous and, one might imagine, pretty uncomfortable fig leaf covering!

In all this all the roles that God had initially established were inverted: the man listened to his wife instead of God, the woman listened to the creature and not her husband. Indeed, whereas it was God who had originally defined the creation as good, here we read that Eve had taken that role upon herself when she decided the fruit of the tree was "good" in v6. And just as the LORD God took a rib from the man to make the woman, now the woman "took" the fruit and gave it to the man. Previously the story had been all about the goodness of God giving the human pair everything they needed; now the human pair were usurping that gracious provision and choosing instead to provide for themselves (including a covering of fig leaves!). The whole story is a tragic reversal of God's grace, which instead of bringing the equality with God that the serpent had suggested they were missing out on, served only to create a terrible division that previously hadn't existed.

The cleverness in the way all this is expressed in such a simple story is truly profound. The act of doing the one thing that they were told not to do served to bring a new force into being which we hereafter describe as "sin". But here we learn that sin isn't just about what we do. By describing it in these verses as something that they took into themselves, sin is seen as being something that becomes part of them. Hereafter, sin was something they *were*![65] It was only after they discovered the difference between good and evil that they knew what 'sin' was. And the result of

---

65 Sin has been defined as an action committed against God. In this story we see that the action of their *eating* the forbidden fruit symbolised their taking that action *into* themselves. Essentially, that rebellion became part of who they were and had the terrible consequence of breaking their relationship both with their maker and between themselves.

this opening of their eyes was the loss of their innocence – their nakedness. Now, instead, they were covered in guilt and shame, and their fig leaves were to be its physical embodiment!

YOU WILL NOT CERTAINLY DIE?

But before we go on, there's another aspect that we need to reflect on. When God had given the instruction to Adam that he should not eat from the tree of the knowledge of good and evil, He had warned him that if he did eat from it, he would certainly die (Genesis 2:17). But the serpent, in tempting the woman to eat the fruit disputed this and told her "you will not certainly die" (Genesis 3:4). We have just read that both the man and the woman chose to ignore God's instructions and listen to the snake and it would appear that he had actually spoken the truth; the man and the woman, having eaten the fruit, didn't die! Or did they?

When God gave that first warning to the man, I wonder what he understood by the idea of death? Had he experienced death at that stage? Certainly, something significant happened to the man and his wife once they had eaten the forbidden fruit. The contentment they had experienced in being naked together was now gone and they sought instead to hide themselves from God and from each other. One might say that their innocence immediately died and so too the intimate relationship they had enjoyed both with God and with each other. We might say of this that they were now 'spiritually' dead even if still physically alive. Indeed, if we read on, when we come to Genesis 5:5 we read a refrain that never needed to be written: 'Altogether, Adam lived a total of 930 years, *and then he died*.' Even if Adam did not experience an immediate physical death, the seed of his rebellion and consequent demise had been sown. Even if the serpent could claim to have given a literal interpretation, it was God's word that ultimately proved to be true.

> So, again, let me pause a moment and ask you to consider this for a moment: what is death? When does it really happen? How would you describe the change in the first human couple after they had eaten the forbidden fruit? Why do you think Jesus often talked about death as being like sleep (have a look at John 11:11-14 as example)?[66] Who really spoke the truth in this situation, God or the serpent?[67]

Then the man and his wife heard the sound of the LORD God as he was walking in the garden in the cool of the day, and they hid from the LORD God among the trees of the garden.   Genesis 3:8

WHERE ARE YOU?

The total transformation resulting from this terrible event is subtly emphasised once more. The trees that God had placed in the garden that were both pleasing to the eye and good for food (Genesis 2:9) took on a new purpose. They provided a hiding

66 On several occasions when Jesus was told that someone had died, he seemed to deny that reality and suggest instead that the person was sleeping (see for example: Luke 8:52).
67 You might find Ephesians 2:1-10 an interesting passage to reflect on.

place for the man and his wife! As Wenham notes: "the trust of innocence is replaced by the fear of guilt."[68] It's actually amazing how doing that which we know we shouldn't do will lead us to feel completely differently. We may all handle it in different ways, but I know for myself that when I have become conscious of doing something wrong, whether deliberately or accidentally, my peace is totally lost and there is a sense that my guilt feels more like a prison. Guilt is a very unforgiving task master!

> I wonder if this is another one of those moments where you might like to pause for a moment and think of a time when you did something wrong, whether intentionally or accidentally, and try to remember how that made you feel at the time (or maybe still feel)? What this amazing incident reveals is not just a very clever exploration into how the subtleties of sin pull us into their trap, but the result of this so often leads us to feeling guilt and shame for our actions and wishing to hide that reality!

Back in the story we note that the man and his wife heard the sound of the LORD God as he was walking in the garden in the cool of the day.

Now, I don't know about you, but I find this verse very interesting for a number of reasons.

Firstly, it makes me wonder what the sound they heard actually was? Was God whistling to himself as he walked along? Did they hear the rustle of his steps? Was this a preincarnate Jesus

68 Wenham, *Genesis 1-15*, p76

that they knew and engaged with? Was this part of God's daily routine; popping in for a chat with his friends when it wasn't quite so hot? The story answers none of these questions; we are left to muse. But I love the idea that God just wanted to see them, to see maybe what they'd been up to. It was probably the first and only time that the man and his wife hadn't been bursting to show the LORD their discoveries and delights. Their absence spoke louder than words. But God came walking anyway as they hid in the trees with their fig leaves for camouflage.

But the LORD God called to the man, "Where are you?" Genesis 3:9

Commentators debate whether this was a genuine question or simply a device to invite the couple to come forth and own up. One thing is certain though, the one who walks in the garden is referred to again as "the LORD God." Ultimately, whatever our actions, it is to the LORD God that we must give an account. And this verse could read, as some have argued, that this is God calling the first human couple to account. Alternatively, and I must say I favour this alternative suggestion, this could also be read as God being gracious once again. Here was a chance for them to come out and to come clean; to come forth and own up to their misdeeds. Their wearing of fig leaves would have been a bit of tell all as to what they had done! I don't think the writer is here concerned with matters of God's omniscience (did he know what they'd done before he asked the question). Rather, this again is a very practical lesson to us all who have made mistakes. God comes looking for us! He made this couple, they were made good, and God knows, we must assume, that the 'crafty snake' is a wily adversary. The question isn't so much about where they are hiding, nor what they have done, so much as what they want to do about it! They have broken the one rule that God gave them and they know they have done wrong; their very act of hiding from God tells them, and Him, that. They have no excuse.

It's also interesting to note that the LORD God 'called to the man' (3:9)! Does the fact that God called to the man rather than to them both infer some difference in the way they related to God? Was this because the man was the one created first and directly by God? Is there an implication that the man had a different responsibility in that he had received the instructions about the forbidden fruit directly from God before the woman was even made from his side? Is this why the serpent spoke directly to the woman rather than the man? The text seems to give this implication even though it is not explicitly stated. However we answer those questions, one thing is clear: the man is the one who God addresses directly. So, how will he respond? Will he accept the responsibility he had and accept the blame for their sorrowful state? We'll soon find out! But before we do, time for another brief detour.

MALE AND FEMALE

Many people, especially I would say in the western world in the twentieth and twenty-first centuries, have struggled with the apparent gender bias found in the Bible. The two key schools of thought about this both have biblical evidence to support their case.

Firstly, there are those who would call themselves 'egalitarians': those who essentially understand the sexes to be completely equal in value and status. The opposing view is known as 'Complementarianism' and is a theological view that men and women have different but complementary roles and responsibilities in marriage, family life, and religious leadership. Whichever way you read the text, what is clear is that it is only as male *and* female that we find that humans are able to fully image God (Genesis 1:27). And it is also clear that the man without his female 'helper' was described for the only time in the creation narrative as being a situation that was 'not good' (Genesis 2:18).

However, it is also interesting that it was to the man, before the creation of his 'helper,' that God gave the instructions regarding the forbidden fruit (Genesis 2:17). So, as we observed, the serpent seemed to exercise an aspect of his craftiness in approaching the woman (Genesis 3:1) and when God came walking in the garden it was the man that he called out to (Genesis 3:9). The whole sequence of the narrative therefore does seem to point to a certain order of things but without any hint of establishing any sort of superiority or added significance. The order of Genesis 2 seems to be: God > man > woman > animals. And it is the reversing of this order that we witness in Genesis 3: the serpent > the woman > the man > God (who appears to be the last to know what has transpired). Maybe it's helpful to consider in these verses how they point us to a bigger narrative.

The man comes from God and is given life by him. Hence, he is the one God gives instructions to. The woman comes from the man and therefore receives God's directives from the man.

But, rather than reading into this any sense of male authority/ dominance, a better consideration might be to read into it a sense of 'covering'. The man is to provide a 'covering' for his wife in that he is responsible for passing on to her the instructions he received from God. And he does seem to have done this. We don't know from the text whether Adam embellished God's instructions that they shouldn't *touch* the forbidden fruit or whether this was simply added by the woman as she was led to doubt God by the serpent. I would suggest the latter, but it is not explicitly stated.

The debate about the relationship between the genders rumbles on over time and it was certainly an issue in the early church.[69] Indeed, it remains somewhat contentious even today. There is not the space here to delve further into the arguments which often seem to come down to interpretations of 'headship' and whether this denotes the man having authority over his wife or whether it refers to his being the *source* of his wife (as in the headwaters of a river).[70] Paul later uses this idea of headship in some very interesting things he has to say about the husband/ wife relationship.[71]

69 1 Timothy 2:12-15
70 For a good analysis of these arguments from an egalitarian perspective I would recommend reading Stanley Grenz's book *Women in the Church*, published by Intervarsity Press, Downers Grove, Illinois, 1995. The complementary position is well documented in John Piper and Wayne Grudem's book *Recovering Biblical Manhood & Womanhood*, published by Crossway Books, Wheaton, Illinois, 1991.
71 Ephesians 5:22-32: Wives, submit yourselves to your own husbands as you do to the Lord. For the husband is the head of the wife as Christ is the head of the church, his body, of which he is the Saviour. Now as the church submits to Christ, so also wives should submit to their husbands in everything. Husbands, love your wives, just as Christ loved the church and gave himself up for her to make her holy, cleansing her by the washing with water through the word, and to present her to himself as a radiant church,

There is something deeply profound and mysterious about the way God designed humans to be male and female and it would be tragic for us to lose our sense of awe over the very fabric of our diversity. Whatever your views on the gender distinctives here, God's call is to the man, as 3:9 makes clear. And it is the man who responds:

He answered, "I heard you in the garden, and I was afraid because I was naked; so I hid." Genesis 3:10

Now another interpretation of this verse reads: "I heard your voice in the garden...". This is interesting because we considered earlier how the voice of God, his 'word', was described in John's gospel as the one who became flesh.[72] This might lend support to the view that it was a preincarnate Jesus who the man encountered walking in the garden. Whether that is the case or not, the man is certainly aware that the one who called to him is the God who speaks to him. And now the man admits that he was afraid. Interestingly, he doesn't say he was afraid because he'd just done the one thing that God had told him not to do. Rather he says he was afraid because he was naked. How often we focus on the practical, tangible outcome and ignore the bigger issue that lies behind it! The irony again is that he would only be afraid of being naked if he'd discovered the knowledge of good and evil by eating the forbidden fruit! And the result

---

without stain or wrinkle or any other blemish, but holy and blameless. In this same way, husbands ought to love their wives as their own bodies. He who loves his wife loves himself. After all, no one ever hated their own body, but they feed and care for their body, just as Christ does the church— for we are members of his body. "For this reason a man will leave his father and mother and be united to his wife, and the two will become one flesh." This is a profound mystery – but I am talking about Christ and the church.

72 John 1:1 & 14

of this action caused him to hide from God because he knew he'd done wrong. It's interesting that the way the man describes this is a reversal of what had actually happened. He heard the LORD God in the garden, he was afraid, because he was naked, so he hid; this actually reverses the whole scenario! Again, the four aspects of this scene mirror the four actions of the woman we noted earlier from verse 6. There, we read of the woman: She saw, she took, she ate and she gave. Now we read of the man: he heard, he was afraid, he was naked and he hid. Thus, the woman's four actions seem to be mirrored in the man's four actions. So how would God deal with this?

God's reply engages directly with the man's reply:

> And he (God) said, "Who told you that you were naked? Have you eaten from the tree that I commanded you not to eat from?" Genesis 3:11

HAVE YOU EATEN FROM THE TREE?

God knows, of course, exactly what has happened, so we might wonder why he still asked the questions?

To answer that I recall a little story from my past. When our nephew and nieces were quite young, they came to stay with us one summer. Now it must be said that I am not especially photogenic, in fact not at all so, but there was one photo of my wife and I that I was quite pleased with and consequently we were willing to have on display. During the visit I noticed to my horror that one of them had added a rather unflattering moustache to the photo in permanent ink completely ruining it. I was somewhat dismayed by this but I wanted to use the opportunity to teach them something about respecting other people's property and how important it is to confess when we do things wrong. So, each child was spoken to in turn and asked to tell us if they were the one who had done this. They were promised that we wouldn't be cross, but it was important to own up if we did something wrong. Try as we might, we couldn't get to the truth of the matter. None of them would own up, but neither were they prepared to point the finger of guilt at another (we'll return to that idea in a moment). I guess, with hindsight, it was probably asking too much to hope that we would get to the truth. But, for me, it spoilt something of the time together that summer as I could never quite trust them after that and anything left on display had to be carefully checked thereafter. What could have been a very liberating lesson in the power of confession and forgiveness served only to diminish our trust and spoil something of the relationship we had together.

So, what has that story to do with Genesis 3:11? I'd say everything.

Unlike us, God knew what the human couple had done: the man has just confessed as much. But here is a chance for Adam to come clean; to own up, to say: "it was me and I am truly sorry". Had he done so I wonder how the story would have gone? There's a beautiful verse in the New Testament that may potentially give us a clue: 1 John 1:9 reads:

If we confess our sins, he is faithful and just and will forgive us our sins and purify us from all unrighteousness.

The key aspect of this is that we need to 'confess our sins'. We need to agree with God that what we've done wasn't right and led to our relationship being damaged. But I love the promise of what God will do if we do this: 'he is faithful and just and will forgive us our sins and purify us from all unrighteousness.' If we confess then God will forgive us of what we've done wrong and make us right again, restoring us to good relationship together. Had our culprit owned up we'd probably have had a good laugh about what they'd done whilst hopefully teaching them that this sort of thing is not acceptable. The fact that the culprit didn't confess served only to spoil things.

So, how will Adam react? Will he confess; his guilt is undeniable!

> The man said, 'The woman you put here with me – she gave me some fruit from the tree and I ate it.'
> Genesis 3:12

NOT MY FAULT

Now, if you think back to the serpent's approach to the woman, what Adam said here is also literally true. God *did* put the woman with him! And she *did* give him some fruit from the tree! But there is no denying his culpability in his final admission: 'and I ate it.' The way that Adam puts it here though, shows him doing that classic action of blaming others for his own wrong-doing and thereby refusing to accept responsibility for his own actions!

First, he seems to be blaming God: 'The woman *you* put here with me'. Forgetting that God graciously gave the woman to be the man's helper to stave off his 'aloneness', Adam seems to suggest that he only ate the fruit because God put at his side someone who would lead him to this action. In other words, Adam says: "I only ate it because YOU God put her with me!"

But if that isn't a sufficient enough excuse, then Adam's next line of defence is to blame her:

'*she gave me some fruit from the tree'*.

In other words, had she not done this then Adam seems to be suggesting he would never have eaten it!

Interestingly, apart from himself, the only one that Adam doesn't seem to blame is the serpent! Once more his utter craftiness in causing this situation with no apparent culpability attached to him is loathsome.

However, what is so sad in all this is the complete lack of contrition from the man. Instead of accepting any responsibility for his actions he seeks to point the finger away from himself. And, if I'm really honest, I too recognize in this something that isn't unique to Adam! If I am caught out, if I am found to have messed up, that tendency to blame others rather than accepting the blame myself can all too easily arise in me. It was actually surprising that when our youngsters were confronted, they didn't seek to do the same and point the finger of guilt at one another!

So, Adam has had his opportunity to do the right thing. But he didn't!

Now before we move on, I wonder if you are willing to do a little introspection too? Does this ring any bells? This action of blaming others when you yourself have done what you knew to be wrong? Is this something you've ever done? I guess none of us likes to be caught out. None of us likes to be in a place where we need to own up to our own failings. Yet to *not* do so, and especially to try and shift the blame to another, is, in itself, another action that compounds our wrongdoing. God offered the man a wonderful opportunity to simply say 'sorry'. It seems to be such a hard word to say, yet so liberating.

So maybe pause a moment and ask yourself, is there someone it would be good to say sorry to? Have there been situations where you have sought to incriminate another for your own wrong deeds? Is that a situation that you should be confessing to the Lord? Think again on that wonderful verse from 1 John 1:9: If we confess our sins, he is faithful and just and will forgive us our sins and purify us from all unrighteousness.

If there is anything to do business with God over and you consider that verse, then let me encourage you to do just that before you move on.

Back to the story, God next turns to the woman. How will she respond to the charge levelled against her?

Then the LORD God said to the woman, "What is this you have done?"

Genesis 3:13

WHAT IS THIS YOU HAVE DONE?

God follows the created order of things. After addressing the man, He now turns to the woman; the one whom the man had been quite happy to implicate. Again, this could be read as God holding her to account, or an excellent opportunity for her to do that which Adam failed to do; or maybe both. How will she respond? Wouldn't it have been amazing if the woman said at this point: "O LORD God, I have been so foolish! I was deceived and my deception led me in turn to lead my husband into wrong doing. I misjudged you and I was wrong. I am truly sorry for what I have done and the affect it has had. Please forgive me." That would have been quite something wouldn't it! But that's not how she replied. Instead, we read:

> The woman said, "The serpent deceived me, and I ate." Genesis 3:13

Once again, the guilty party seeks to shift the blame away from herself and on to another; in this case the serpent: "The serpent deceived me, and I ate." In so doing, what we end up with is a completely inverted spoiling of the created order. God > man > woman > animals (here represented by the serpent) becomes instead: serpent > woman > man > God. And the result of this inversion is completely catastrophic. At every stage, the relationships are now spoiled. No one comes out of this well; except, perhaps, the serpent! Whatever his reasons for causing this haemorrhage in the created order, they aren't explicitly stated. But he has succeeded in breaking the intimate bond that previously existed between God and his most loved human creatures. Not only so, but he has succeeded in spoiling the once beautiful relationship between them. Now instead of their shame-free nakedness, they sought to hide themselves from each other and God by their own pathetic remedy of a fig-leaf covering.

Effectively, the serpent has successfully persuaded the human couple to give their authority, as God's regents over creation, to him. When they did the very thing that God told them not to do, and rather did the thing that the serpent had so subtly drawn them into doing, they effectively made him their overseer rather than God. Now it would be the serpent who was *de facto* god of the created order. And he'd been given that position by the very ones who were made for it. The dramatic succession of a new order had been sealed. There has been, in effect, a bloodless coup. Albeit 'blood' would soon be necessary to restore a right order of things. And all this has happened with the compliance of the very ones who were given the role of imaging God. They had now effectively exchanged that image for a crafty, conniving, schemer. We become like those we listen to. In this instance, how *tragic*!

BECAUSE YOU HAVE DONE THIS

But just in case we thought that the crafty serpent had got away with this scot-free, we next read of God addressing *him*! In His response to the serpent, however, unlike his approach to the humans, there is no questioning. It seems unnecessary for God to seek contrition from him as He had Adam and his wife. It seems that *however* it was that the serpent took on this 'form' of being a thorn in God's side, God knows that all opportunities for confession and repentance have passed. All that is left for the serpent is God's verdict and the speaking out of the consequences of his assault on creation:

So the LORD God said to the serpent, "Because you have done this...."

Genesis 3:14a

At last we arrive at the point where there are no half-truths, no deceit, no shifting of blame, no building a case. God, as judge, will now pronounce his verdict and the sentences that fit the crime. Again, with the use of His fuller title: the LORD God, the true essence of God's being is pronounced. He, and only He, is able to pronounce judgement, because, despite the serpent's manoeuvrings, it is the LORD God, and only He, as the creator of the heavens and the earth, who can act as judge over all that He has made. And that includes the serpent. In giving Adam and his wife freewill, God allowed them the potential to rebel against Him and, sadly, they did so. We'll find out what the true consequences of that action will be in a moment. But the real villain is the scheming serpent who deceived them into doing so in the first place. So what will God say to him?

"Cursed are you above all livestock and all wild animals!
You will crawl on your belly and you will eat dust all the days of your life.
And I will put enmity between you and the woman, and between your offspring and hers;
He will crush your head, and you will strike his heel."

Genesis 3:14b-15

Up to this point, God had only spoken blessings over that which

He has made. But now that the humans have discovered the knowledge of good *and evil*, they will also observe that blessings too have their corollary. God's desire is to bless: but where there is rebellion against His will, there is necessarily a contra-outcome. The serpent, who is given no opportunity to make his own excuses, is to receive in himself a punishment that fits his crime. Whilst God sought to bless, the serpent sought to prevent that blessing and will receive into himself the consequence of his so-doing: he will be 'cursed'.

But what does being cursed mean? Wenham says: 'In the bible, to curse is the antonym of to bless. It means to invoke God's judgement on someone, usually for a particular offence'. Those cursed may expect all kinds of misfortune to befall them.'[73] Moreover, because it is God Himself who pronounces the curse, its effectiveness is completely guaranteed. So, what is to be the consequence of his action that the serpent will experience for his rebellious treachery? God's verdict reads like poetry but in every instance the punishment decreed fits the crime:

THE PUNISHMENT FITS THE CRIME

The serpent was introduced in 3:1 as more 'crafty' than all the other wild animals. Now, because of what it has done, it is to be more 'cursed' than all the livestock and all the wild animals 3:14. The serpent sought to place himself above the other creatures, even above the humans and, to some extent, he even sought to usurp God. Now his punishment is to be below them. It is

73 Wenham, *Genesis 1-15,* p78.

so often the case that when God does execute judgements, the punishment exactly fits the nature of the crime: so here. The serpent sought to elevate himself. Now he will find himself lowered to the status of crawling on his belly and in so doing 'eating dust'. Again, the cleverness of this is profound. The serpent ruined the relationship between God and the human pair (the man having been formed from the dust Genesis 2:7) by persuading them to eat that which was forbidden them. Now the serpent is described as 'eating dust' as it crawls along the ground all the days of its life. But I suspect there is more to this than that. In 3:19, as part of the judgement God makes upon the man we read: By the sweat of your brow you will eat your food until you return to the ground, (there's that eating idea again) since from it you were taken; for dust you are and to dust you will return. The serpent had indeed led the woman and her husband to disobey God and listen to him. In effect they gave their God-given authority to the serpent. But if the serpent thought this would give him the right to rule over them then that right would literally only be given in their eventual return to the dust from which they came. As God ruled over life, the serpent's rule would be over the dead (their dust). That would be his realm!

However, there would be another consequence of the actions of the serpent:

And I will put enmity between you and the woman, and between your offspring and hers;
He will crush your head, and you will strike his heel.

HE WILL CRUSH YOUR HEAD, AND YOU WILL STRIKE HIS HEEL

Not only would the serpent be cursed in this way but, having deceived the woman, as she herself stated (3:13), now there would be a deep-rooted hatred, 'enmity', between the woman and the serpent. Indeed, this would pass on down the generations, 'between your offspring and hers'. The serpent's main target seemed to have been his own creator, God, and he had used the humans as his means of attack. But their joint rebellion against God served to create an enmity between themselves. From this point on there would always be hostility between the line of humans and the serpent's line. Yet there is also a hint that this hostility will come to a final climax at some future time: He will crush your head, and you will strike his heel.

With the arrival of the serpent in Genesis 3, we noted that the villain in the story had arrived on the scene. The hint in this verse is that there would come a time when there would also enter a hero, one who would take on the villain and put things right. As we read verse 15 we encounter a very important promise that we would do well to take particular notice of. Essentially, we have read how there will be an ongoing war of sorts from this time forth between the offspring of the humans and the offspring of the serpent as a result of this dastardly deception. But this verse acts as a form of prophecy: there would ultimately come a time when a descendent of the woman, one of her offspring (interestingly the man is not mentioned), will finally crush the serpent's head. We considered earlier, in relation to the male/female relationship, the difficulty in unpacking the real meaning of 'headship'. But to my mind, this is a case where a glorious double meaning is found.

As this curse is spoken over the serpent, we are reminded that the serpent will henceforth be restricted to crawling along the ground. That situation in life will leave it vulnerable to *literally* having its head crushed by a human being, an offspring of the woman. But, if we consider too that sense that 'headship' may also have some meaning of authority or potentially covering, this verse also suggests that any authority over the humans that the serpent has acquired through his deception will ultimately be removed. Again with a potential double-meaning included, this victory will come at a cost to the human victor, the hero of the story. From its lowly position, the serpent will be ideally placed to strike the very heel of the human as he strikes his victory blow. The one who delivers the devastating blow to the serpent's head also seems to receive in himself a critical wound. In other words, the ultimate human victory here seems to come only at terrible cost. The bite of a serpent often carries with it a deadly venom. Given that this battle takes place within the context of the making known the twin aspects of good and evil, we could even say that this verse seems to suggest that whilst good will ultimately triumph it will only be when evil strikes its cruellest, most deadly, evil blow.

THE GOD OF PEACE WILL SOON CRUSH SATAN UNDER YOUR FEET

Now before we go on, we might note that this phrase also occurs in the Apostle Paul's masterpiece of theological explanation that we know as the letter of Romans. In Romans 16:20, among Paul's final greetings, we read: The God of peace will soon crush Satan under your feet.

How interesting that Paul would see the work of the Christians in Rome as in some way connected to the fulfilment of this prophecy. There are a number of interesting things about it that we might note:

Firstly, when Paul uses this idea of one being crushed under foot, he actually speaks not of a serpent, but Satan, the enemy of God now fully unmasked as the accuser. This is certainly a hint that the true identity of the serpent we encounter in Genesis 3 is none other than Satan.

Secondly, Paul suggests that Satan will be crushed under your feet, that is the feet of the followers of Christ.

But, thirdly, it is the God of peace who will be the one who brings about this crushing *through* them. And, of course, it was Jesus who came to bring peace between God and humankind and he achieved that goal through his substitutionary death on the cross. For *that* was the moment the venom of the serpent did its deadly worst.

All this suggests that by the time Paul was writing he had come to understand that Genesis 3:15 was pointing forward prophetically to the work of Christ making peace once more between humans and their maker. And he did this by destroying the works of the one who had caused the true division between them, the serpent, who was in fact none other than Satan himself. At the moment that he struck his deadliest blow against the offspring of the woman (though not the seed of the man incidentally), he was simultaneously crushing the head of the serpent and setting free the human captives that he had ensnared. Thus Genesis 3:15 found its ultimate fulfilment in that head crushing, heel biting moment. And because God was the one who announced this curse upon the serpent (Genesis 3:14-15) there was no doubting its fulfilment. The serpent had been given notice that his time would come.

TO THE WOMAN, GOD SAID

Having delivered his verdict towards the serpent, God next turned his attention to the woman who had been deceived. Now it was time for her to hear the verdict against her. However, just before we do, we need to note one very important thing: though her actions had been in direct contradiction to the instructions she had received, God did *not* speak a curse over her. God knew who the true originator of the broken relationship was, and *he* had now received his curse. The woman, however, remained under God's blessing; that would not be rescinded despite her actions. But what she had done had brought a new dimension to the human story. She had chosen to turn her back on the goodness and grace of God and that could only lead to tragic consequences.

To the woman he (God) said,

> "I will make your pains in childbearing very severe; with painful labour you will give birth to children.
> Your desire will be for your husband, and he will rule over you."

> Genesis 3:16

The golden rule when it comes to judgement in the Bible seems to be that the punishment fits the crime. So, as God turns to address the woman, still not named individually at this point, we need to consider afresh what her role was and what she actually did wrong if we are to understand God's judgement.

We remember that the man being alone was the only defective element of the creation narrative. None of the other animals was found to be a suitable helper for him. God had blessed the man and called him to be fruitful but he couldn't achieve this task alone, nor could he truly image God, who was in himself a community of oneness, if he was alone. So God had taken from the man a rib and from that rib God had made the woman to be his helper; not subordinate to him but to fulfil him. She alone, as taken from him, was equal to him in essence; together they could now both image their maker more effectively and provide the means for their fruitfulness as commanded by God. They were offered unlimited access to all the fruits of their garden paradise, including the fruit from the tree of life. Yet God had told the man and he, in turn it seemed, had told his wife that they were not allowed to eat from the tree of the knowledge of good and evil. Yet, as the serpent had deceived the woman, she had eaten of it; not only so but she'd given some to her husband and he had eaten too. Thus, just as the woman had done the one thing God had commanded them not to do, so the one thing that only she could do, to bear children, would now become a source of pain. God was not cursing the woman but he did disrupt her appointed role.

Again, there is a play on words here in the original language that we miss in our English translations. The closest we can get to this is to say something along the lines of the 'tree' brought 'trauma'.[74] In other words, by turning her back on God's good desires for her 'work', she had now made that work that much more difficult and painful. We should note here that this was *not* God's intention, nor his desire for the woman. But the act of justice denotes that, as God truly values us, our actions do have consequences. The first consequence of the woman's rejection of God's word would have implications for the future of every subsequent human birth.

However, the woman's action had another aspect to it: she not only *ate* the forbidden fruit herself, but she *gave* some to her husband and he ate too (3:6). Now we mentioned earlier the differences of opinion relating to the relationship between the man and the woman before this rebellion took place. There are those who see (pre-fall) an aspect of the man having 'authority' over his wife as he had already called her 'woman'. Whereas others suggest that it was God who had thus called her this and the man was simply using the same term. They suggest, instead, no aspect of authority between them but a complete mutuality of relationship. Others perceive though that, in the giving of the instructions to the man prior to the creation of the woman, and in His calling out to the man rather than the woman when they hid from him, God is exercising some degree of differentiation between them. Whatever your conclusion to this, the next aspect of God's verdict upon the woman is once again a clear example of the punishment fitting the crime.

It was the woman who had led the man into sin by giving him the fruit to eat. He was, of course, responsible for his own actions

74 Wenham, *Genesis 1-15*, p81

and he will get his turn to face the judge next. But instead of listening to and obeying God's instruction, given through the man, the woman had led him to do the opposite. Therefore, the second aspect of her judgement is that henceforth her 'desire will be for your husband and he will rule over you.' Instead of the mutuality of existence they had known prior to their sin, now there would be a breaking of their prior bond so that she will now be subject to male domination.

By not adhering to God's covering over her, through her husband whereby she was able to learn of God's very particular instruction, she would now be subject not to his covering but his domination. She had wanted him to join her in her sinful action: she wanted him rather than wanting to do that which pleased God. Henceforth, she would continue to desire her husband over above God. Because this is so *not* what God had set up in the created order for His beloved humans, life will never be as rich or fulfilling as it would otherwise have been.

Throughout history this reality can be seen working its way out in human society. What this looks like differs across the world but there are so many gender injustices that exist which all find their roots in this terrible scene in the garden.

JESUS TURNS THE GENDER TIDE

Before we go on to hear what God had to say to Adam, I think it is worth pausing to consider the radically different approach to gender relations that Jesus exhibited. As I mentioned earlier, I absolutely love it that the first person to see the risen Lord Jesus after his resurrection was a woman. In those days a women's testimony was not acceptable as a witness in a legal setting. Here we see that the first witness to God's work of redemption was a woman who ran and told her male fellow disciples. This is phenomenal. Similarly, it was Jesus' mother Mary who brought Jesus into the world with no direct involvement from Joseph. In both instances I see God overturning the gender imbalances as He began his work of realigning the fallen world to be more in tune with his original design.

I love it too that when Jesus promised that His Holy Spirit would be poured forth on the church at the start of the new era we read:

"In the last days, God says, I will pour out my Spirit on all people.
Your sons and daughters will prophesy, your young men will see visions, your old men will dream dreams.
Even on my servants, both men and women, I will pour out my Spirit in those days, and they will prophesy...."

Acts 2:17-18.

There are gender distinctives between male and female but in God's kingdom both male and female will receive the Spirit of God. There remains something deeply profound about the way the union of a husband and a wife points to the ultimate union God seeks between himself (Jesus the bridegroom) and the church (his bride). But we should be in no doubt, God did not seek this gender imbalance. Rather, He longs that women too should sit at his feet as his disciples on the same basis as men.[75]

75 See for example the story of Mary and Martha in Luke 10:38-42

It was now the man's turn to hear what God would say to him:

> To Adam he said, "Because you listened to your wife and ate fruit from the tree about which I commanded you, 'You must not eat from it,'
> "Cursed is the ground because of you; through painful toil you will eat food from it all the days of your life. It will produce thorns and thistles for you, and you will eat the plants of the field. By the sweat of your brow you will eat your food until you return to the ground, since from it you were taken; for dust you are and to dust you will return."
> Genesis 3:17-19

TO ADAM HE SAID

Once more God does not curse the man, Adam. However, the ground from which he came is now cursed. Oh, how easy Adam had had it before. In the Garden Paradise, food was freely and easily obtainable and the fruit trees that surrounded them produced a constant supply of food. Yet somehow, with all that choice and all that ease, Adam still listened to his wife rather than God. And as you may have picked up already, the punishment he faced would be a direct response to what he'd done. If easily and freely available food wasn't enough for him then henceforth gathering his food would be a whole other story.

God turned to Adam, a name which means something like 'ground' or 'earth,' and gave his verdict.[76] Adam had chosen to

---

76 I love the fact that when God speaks to his first human he names him Adam meaning 'ground' or 'earth'. Then when Jesus gives a new name to his commander-in-chief, Simon, he changes his name to Peter meaning 'rock'. Does this symbolise that the new humanity he is about to build is to be altogether more robust than the first (Mathew 7:24-27)?

listen to his wife rather than to God. This was his fundamental mistake: he had his priorities wrong. As if to make the point crystal clear, five times in these three verses God reminds Adam that his sin was connected directly to what he had eaten. Adam's offence consisted of eating the forbidden fruit. Therefore he is punished in the way he will subsequently have to work hard to provide his food to eat. Whereas God had placed Adam in a well-watered garden, a blessed place where produce grew easily, now the land itself would be cursed.

The whole section spoken by God to Adam is bracketed by the ground. God initially pronounces the curse on the ground and concludes his remarks to Adam by reminding him that he came from the dust/ground and that it's to that which he would ultimately return. Both the man and his wife would now endure 'painful toil'. She in bearing children, he in his role as the one who supplies their food.

But there is another subtle note here. The serpent had suggested that if the woman and her husband did eat of the forbidden fruit they would not die, despite God telling them they would. Now God tells Adam that it would only be through painful toil that he would be able to provide food 'all the days of your life.' The clear inference of this is that, henceforth, the lives of the humans would be limited. God's promise of death if they chose to ignore Him would ultimately be found to be true.

There is another sad contrast in this section to what we observed in Genesis 2. In 2:9 we read how the LORD God made all kinds of trees grow out of the ground – trees that were pleasing to the eye and good for food. Now we read that the ground 'will produce thorns and thistles for you and you will eat the plants of the field' (3:18). The reference to the thorns and thistles that would come forth from the ground of the field, or plain, also hints that, having turned away from God's provision and chosen their own, the human couple could no longer stay within God's garden and would now need to leave the garden to cultivate the plain to provide their food. But now, instead of knowing God with them, His blessing upon them, they had chosen a path that He had not desired for them. By rejecting His blessing they had instead chosen for themselves a cursed path and thus the fruitful trees that God provided would now be replaced by vegetation that would oppose their efforts. From this time on their food would only be grown 'by the sweat of your brow' (3:19). Again, the contrast with Genesis 2 is notable. Work was not a new thing. Adam was placed in the garden to 'work the ground and take care of it' (2:15). Work was an original part of his wholesome, healthy humanity. It wouldn't be difficult. But now that work would be hard and frustrating.

For both the woman and the man, their choice of effective independence from God did not lead to the freedom they had supposed but rather to frustration and difficulty. Just as the woman would suffer in the bringing forth of the fruit of her womb, so the man would suffer in the bringing forth of fruit from the earth. Both of these consequences are the direct result of them taking into themselves the forbidden fruit. The life-long struggle to survive would eventually lead to death just as God had said. Man was formed from the dust of the ground (2:7) and he would eventually return to that same dust (2:19). Just as their expulsion from the garden was hinted at in the reference to their toil of the plain rather than their continued existence within the garden, so the suggestion that the man would eventually return to the dust suggests that their access to the tree of life would soon be curtailed too.

Instead of Adam being ruler over the ground as God initially intended him to be, these verses suggest that instead the ground would to some extent rule over mankind. But not forever! So, before we continue, I want to input one aspect of hope into this sorry tale.

A CROWN OF VICTORY

Do you remember what happened to Jesus as he was being prepared for his crucifixion?

John 19:2 reads: 'The soldiers twisted together a crown of thorns and put it on his head.' Jesus spoke of his moment of crucifixion as the moment when His Kingdom was being inaugurated. The cross became the throne upon which the world's true king was installed. Even the sign above his head declared it for all the world to read (John 19:19). So, what was the crown that Jesus wore? Not a crown that we are used to seeing new monarchs wear. For Jesus, that crown was a crown of *thorns*. I love that image. To my mind, this reverses the tragic scene that stands before us in Genesis 3:18. When Jesus, the new Adam (see 1 Corinthians 15:45-48), was inaugurated as king, His crown demonstrated something deeply profound. That which once had been *under* Adam, had subsequently been elevated *over* Him. In the death of Jesus, though, there was a new reversal. That which had been to Adam's shame was now a sign of Christ's victory. The thorns which had been the sign of Adam's failure would now be a symbol of Christ's victory!

God had spoken. The damage had been done. The consequences of Adam and his wife doing that which God had expressly told them not to do had begun to work their way out. Having effectively rejected God, the human pair had been given the freedom and autonomy that their actions had so clearly demonstrated that they sought. But, having turned away from the God who's nature was so clearly to seek to bless, they would now have to accept life outside His direct blessing. But the great story of God's plan would not be completely thwarted. The serpent had won a key victory but he hadn't won the war!

HOPE AFTER ALL

After such a devastating sequence of judgements, as we turn to verse 20 there is an element of hope. Adam named his wife Eve, because she would become the mother of all the living. Having eaten the fruit that God said would lead to death, it's quite something that Adam would name his wife Eve, because she would become the mother of all the living! But in the judgements that God had given against both Adam and his wife, there had been no hint of immediate death, even if there was the distinct suggestion that their days would now be numbered (3:19).

Some commentators note that the name 'Eve' is similar to the Aramaic word 'serpent' and therefore the suggestion is made that in naming her this, Adam is rebuking his wife for deceiving him by effectively calling her "serpent".[77]

However, the addition of the stated reason clause, because she would become the mother of all the living, suggests otherwise to me. Whether or not Adam did 'name' his wife earlier when he referred to her as 'woman' (2:23), he certainly names her at this juncture. And as we noted earlier the act of naming another is understood as exercising some sense of dominion over them. So here is Adam effectively doing that which God had judged would happen when he spoke his judgement over the woman in 3:16. Her name does define her role, albeit a more painful one (3:16). From Eve would eventually come every single human being who would be born on earth; therefore, she is rightly called the mother of all the living. But sadly, having now rebelled against her maker and led her husband to do the same, she would now be the mother of a race of human beings who are no longer able to enjoy the innocence of nakedness that they once had (2:25). From this time on, human beings would know *only* the outcome of their disobedience to God: the resulting guilt and shame would be part of the inheritance they would now pass on.

COVERING THEIR SHAME: AT GREAT COST

The next verse is another incredibly important verse that could be so easily missed. In some ways, it goes on to explain so much

---

77 Wenham, *Genesis 1-15*, p.84

of the practices of ancient Israel that will be covered in the next books of the Bible and point forward to God's ultimate act of reversal to this dreadful calamity:

The LORD God made garments of skin for Adam and his wife and clothed them
Genesis 3:21

You will remember that as soon as the human pair had eaten the forbidden fruit, they had effectively discovered what it meant to disobey God. And in so-doing, they had discovered the difference between good and evil. (I defined evil as essentially doing that which we know God had said 'no' to). That action caused them to discover terrible new sensations that hitherto they had not known: guilt and shame! Prior to this discovery, they had had nothing to be ashamed about and were described as being naked and feeling no shame (2:25). But as soon as they had broken God's one single rule then their guilt had led them to become aware of their nakedness and seek to hide it behind their own coverings of fig-leaves (3:7). The shear ridiculous impracticality of such coverings would be all too apparent. But in this verse we discover something of the utter grace of God, together with a sign-post to how God would eventually deal with their shameful predicament!

To begin with we must ask the obvious question: where did God get the garments of skin to clothe them? The only answer can be from the death of an animal whose skin God used. It's important to remember here that God had said that if the human couple ate from the tree of the knowledge of good and evil they would certainly die (2:17). Now the serpent disputed this and persuaded the woman to eat anyway, which she did and her husband too. Indeed, they hadn't immediately died but the text suggests that their situation had certainly changed and that their physical death would now become a reality even if not an immediate one. So, how was it that their immediate death was avoided? In this verse we meet one of the most amazing acts of God's grace that could be imagined. There was a substitution!

The discovery of good and evil, we might say of life *and death*, meant a change to the created order. We might reflect that initially the human diet was entirely vegetarian. There had been no death recorded in the story up until this point. But now, with good *and evil* out in the open, God used the death of an animal as a means of 'covering' the shame of the first human pair. Their covering of vegetation would not be sufficient. Now, the only way for their lives to continue would be because of the substitutionary death of another living creature. And that creature's skin would be the means of covering the humans both physically, to hide their shame, and at a deeper level, spiritually.

The death of the animal in their place is the first recorded act of sacrifice in the Bible. A life was shed, and that life became their substitute and provided the necessary covering for their sin and shame. It was the means of God being both true to his word (that death would follow their rejection of His word) and yet maintain His desire to have a relationship with the humans who were made in his image. One way of describing this process would be skin for skin!

However, there is another aspect of this that we also ought to comment on before we move on. Wenham notes that the expression 'clothed them' is used later in the Bible to describe the dress either of a king (as an example: 1 Samuel 17:38) or for the dressing of the priests in their sacred vestments (as in Leviticus 8:13).[78] In this way, the language of the garden runs parallel with the worship practices of Israel. The detailed arrangements of how the Israelites were to dress in order to worship God paid particular attention to how dangerous it was to be around God when they came as sinful people. In Exodus 20:26, they had to ensure they were dressed in such a way as to maintain their modesty and not reveal their nakedness to God. Like light effectively destroying darkness, for those who now live in the darkness of their sin, to approach the light that is God, is tantamount to self-destruction. Thus, the clothing of Adam and Eve by God, the effective covering of their guilt and shame, at this juncture might point forward to that too. Although their nakedness was now covered, their dress reminded them that they came to God as those marred by sin.

All of this leads me to another detour! When Jesus was crucified, his robes were taken from him and guards played dice to keep them (Matthew 27:35). Despite the many historical paintings of Jesus hanging on the cross with a loincloth covering, it was the usual Roman practice to crucify the condemned naked as an additional act of shaming them before the might of Rome. As Jesus hung naked on that Roman cross, this was to be the ultimate act of substitution. He gave his skin for us!

When Jesus was introduced in John's gospel by his cousin, John the Baptist, he said of him: "Look the Lamb of God, who takes

78 Wenham, *Genesis 1-15*, p84

away the sin of the world!"[79] What an amazing proclamation. John recognized Jesus as the one who would become the ultimate fulfilment of Genesis 3:21. Here was the one who would crush the head of the serpent (Genesis 3:15) by laying down his own life in sacrifice. Here was the one whose heal the serpent would bite (Genesis 3:15). God provided the sacrifice in the garden (Genesis 3:21) and God would indeed provide the ultimate sacrifice in His own Son (John 1:29). Jesus would be crucified naked though He had done no evil, even though He had done nothing wrong (Luke 23:41). Jesus had nothing whatsoever to be ashamed of but He took upon himself our shame and took the death that should be ours and let it run its course in Himself.

Boom!

The whole Christian good news stems from this. We are all born of Eve, the mother of all the living (Genesis 3:20). We are all born in that line of sin and shame (Romans 3:23). But Jesus Christ died as our substitute to take our sin and shame upon himself so that through faith in him we might be forgiven and set free from the curse of death and restored to right relationship with God (2 Corinthians 5:21). Now if that isn't a 'boom' moment I don't know what is!!

When we do things wrong, there is often guilt and shame but there are also usually consequences involved. In the same way, if we step away from God's good plan, how can there not be. So, next in our account we will hear what those consequences were going to be:

79 John 1:29

ACTIONS HAVE CONSEQUENCES

And the LORD God said, "The man has now become like one of us, knowing good and evil. He must not be allowed to reach out his hand and take also from the tree of life and eat, and live forever." Genesis 3:22

When God says the man has now become like one of us, we are back to that question we posed earlier: who does He mean by "us"? To answer that we need to ponder who, at this moment in the story, knew what that difference actually was? And one party to that knowledge was indeed the serpent! Part of his temptation to the woman had been that if she defied God's instructions and ate the forbidden fruit, she would become like God in that she would then know that difference between good and evil; this was something she hadn't known before, despite being made in his image. The implication here then is that the serpent already knew that difference! Thus we are given to understand that the knowing of good and evil, as well as being known to God, seems to have been known by other 'spiritual' beings. Satan in the guise of the serpent was one of them.

Now, interestingly, God is once again directing his attention towards the man rather than the woman. There is very definitely a differentiation being made in the way the writer records God's interactions towards them here. Having received God's instructions directly from Him there is a level of responsibility the man has that God does not seem to attribute to his wife. However, now that Adam has demonstrated his propensity to eat from *any* tree, if his wife should lead him to do so, even the fruit of the only tree that was off-limits, God now issues a new prohibition: "He must not be allowed to reach out his hand and take also from the tree of life and eat, and live forever."

So much in this story has to be read between the lines, seemingly, as often from what is *not* said as well as from what *is*. When God made his original declarations, about what the man could eat and not eat, we read only this: "You are free to eat from any tree in the garden; but you must not eat from the tree of the knowledge of good and evil" (2:16-17). Thus, although it wasn't specifically stated, the inference was that the man could eat from the tree of life, and thus live forever. That, it seemed, was God's intended purpose for the humans: to enjoy an uninterrupted life with God in the very paradise that God had supplied for them. But now that paradise had been marred. The humans had discovered what it meant to live outside of God's will and that knowledge and caused guilt and shame to enter their experience, leaving them in a less-than-paradisical state. And God did not want that situation to be left unchecked forever. So, having provided the means for them to avoid a premature physical death, even if something of a relational, could we call it 'spiritual,' death had already taken place, God needed to act to ensure that this situation did not remain the case indefinitely. The man's access to the tree of life would need to be curtailed.

So the LORD God banished him from the Garden of Eden to work the ground from which he had been taken. Genesis 3:23

We probably miss another clever Hebraic word play in this verse since "reach out" (v22) comes from the same root as "sent out" (banished). Again, this is another instance where the effective punishment directly fits the crime. Adam, and of course Eve, are 'sent out' from where they originally belonged because they had sought to 'reach out' to that which they shouldn't. By so doing God stopped them 'reaching out' to that which he had originally intended them to have access. They cannot be allowed to live forever in this broken state. Even if God's plan remains that they should eventually have access to that 'tree of life' and be with him forever, they cannot be allowed to in their current brokenness.

One last aside, if I may, is to say how I really love it that the ultimate 'tree of life' is the cross of Christ. Here we see God's supreme revelation of His wisdom. When those who place their trust in the Saviour who died there, they do indeed regain their access that tree of life and so to life in all its fulness now and life that also goes on forever!

FORWARD MOTION

In addition, whereas God's plan seemed to be that the man would spread the goodness of the garden paradise beyond the borders of Eden (Genesis 2:5), so now that plan would still proceed as the man was banished from Eden to work the ground. The only, albeit significant, difference now was that the ground that would have worked with him was now cursed (3:17) and worked against him: his rule over it would now be so much more difficult.

This wouldn't have been an altogether enticing prospect. The human pair might well have been sent out, but I suspect, all too

soon, they would be seeking re-entry to the garden paradise.[80]
This could not be allowed to happen. And so we read:

> After he drove the man out, he placed on the east side of the Garden of Eden cherubim and a flaming sword flashing back and forth to guard the way to the tree of life.
> Genesis 3:24

Remembering who it was that created the physical landscape of
the earth, the LORD God could not allow the couple to remain
in Eden and have access to the tree of life. At one level the man
was 'sent out' (banished) from the garden (3:23) but we read
He also 'drove the man out' (3:24). This stronger term was also
used to describe the expulsion of the inhabitants of Canaan who
corrupted that land in Exodus 23:28-31. There is here a sense
of forward motion in the text here. Thus, the story continues
onwards but contains within it a sadness that the humans have
brought this unnecessary hardship upon themselves and must
bear the penalty on into their new circumstances. There is now
no going back. And in case they thought to try, God places a
very effective guard on duty.

NO WAY BACK

The word we read as 'placed', or 'stationed' in some versions,
literally means "caused to camp" and is found elsewhere in
the Bible in situations where God camps among his people

---

80 God's people often had a hankering to return to situations they considered
more acceptable than their current environment even when they were clearly
mistaken. See, for example, Exodus 16:3.

(for example Exodus 25:8).[81] There is a guard on duty who isn't going anywhere, and what a guard it is! The inclusion of a cherubim comes as quite a jarring shock in the story. We shouldn't be mistaken into thinking of the popularised picture of a cherub as a fat baby with a halo! In the Ancient Near East, cherubim were fierce human-headed winged lions who were thought to guard holy places: terrifying warriors. Later in Israel's history, pictures of them adorned the walls of the temple (1 Kings 6:29), and a pair of solid gold cherubim formed the throne of God on the ark of the Covenant (Exodus 25:18-22). These were God's crack troops and the man wasn't about to get past them.

Further, if that wasn't enough of a deterrent, God also put in place a flaming sword flashing back and forth. Whatever picture this conjures up in your mind, the various components sound a little like something found in an Indiana Jones adventure! The fact that the sword is flaming, suggests that it is on fire and fire is often a biblical symbol for God's presence in judgement. A sword flashing back and forth, suggests the inability of *anyone* to get past it without suffering the consequences. And if that sword is in the hands of an angelic warrior, then the way back to the garden seems consequently off-limits!

But why would the way be blocked on the east side? Whenever the Bible speaks of God's presence in either His tabernacle or the temple, the entrance is found on the East side. So, the likelihood is that this protection was placed at the *entrance* to the garden or, in Adam and Eve's case, at the *exit*. There was now

81 Wenham, *Genesis 1-15*, p86

no way back to the tree of life; the fruit of which had been freely available before is now totally out of reach.

With that thought in mind we come to the close of the prologue of the Bible story. Yet we can see that, built into the very closing of it, we are drawn in to the much larger story that is propelled forwards: these first three chapters really only serve to set the scene.

EPILOGUE

Since the beginning, we have been questioning what type of literature we are reading when we look at this fascinating introduction to the world's best-selling book: the Bible. The main arguments about the first chapters of Genesis have often related to how what we read in them relates to scientific discoveries about the beginnings of our world. But as we have read Genesis 1-3 carefully now, it doesn't appear to set out a scientific approach to creation as a key concern. As we said earlier, it isn't so much interested in the 'how' as the 'why' of creation.

So, can we regard these three chapters as, in any sense, historical? Our discoveries certainly seem to suggest a certain amount of historicity. However, I wonder if a better term might be that they contain 'proto-history'; what we have in Genesis 1-3 isn't so much history as detailing for us what came *before* history. This is the background to history, which we might describe better as 'his-story' as it tells the story of God and his relationship to the humans who were supposed to make him known to creation.

Some commentators have read in these chapters a critique of other creation stories and seen in it a polemic against other ancient narratives. Again, I would have to say that various common themes might suggest an element of this without it necessarily being its main purpose. Having seen what we have about the way the writer uses wonderfully creative techniques of word plays and structure, of poetry and subtlety, it might be impossible to contain this work of art in any one single definition.

As the title of *this* book suggests, my interpretation of the first three chapters of Genesis is that they form a wonderful prologue to a much larger narrative which begins as humanity embarks on life outside the paradise that served as their nursery. Genesis 1-3 has so much to tell us about our own nature and that unique combination that we are of breath-taking glory and abject foolishness.

It is my sincere belief that when we set aside our anachronistic questions and allow the story itself to help shape our understanding, we will discover things far more important and profound than simply how old the planet is. Rather, what this prologue does is to inform each successive generation of humans about the most fundamental issues that we need to know for life.

In these beautifully simple yet profound stories we discover The One who made the creation and who put humanity in charge of ruling over it on His behalf. We discover the true nature of our humanity as male and female and why it is that all our relationships are a mixture of beauty and brokenness. We are also given hope that despite the apparent brokenness there is the possibility that the Creator has not abandoned Project Creation; indeed, He has promised to continue to act within the story to bring about a complete reversal of the brokenness that humans brought upon themselves. Further, God promises that the one who stood opposed to Him and used the human beings as his instruments of destruction will eventually be brought to judgement, even at great cost to God Himself.

This is a promise of ultimate hope, of ultimate love, of final triumph. The prologue thus introduces the greatest story ever told, the story that we all find ourselves a part of whether we realise it or not. This is our story and it rolls forward each day as we get to write another part! Let us hold true to the hope and enjoy the journey.

BIBLIOGRAPHY

Bilezikian, G., *Community 101*, Grand Rapids, Michigan: Zondervan, 1997

Hawkey, R., *Healing the Human Spirit*, Chichester, West Sussex: New Wine Press, 2004

Lennox, J.C., *Seven Days that divide the World*, Grand Rapids, Michigan: Zondervan, 2011

Mc Farlane, G., *Why Do You Believe what you believe about the Holy Spirit?*, Carlisle, Cumbria: Pateroster Press, 1998

Piper, J and Grudem, W., *Recovering Biblical Manhood & Womanhood*, Wheaton, Illinois: Crossway Books, 1991

Wenham, G.J., *Genesis 1-15: Word Biblical Commentary*, Waco, Texas: Word, 1987

ABOUT THE AUTHOR

When John Sainsbury met Jesus in his early 20s, it *changed everything*. After a 16-year career in banking, John went to London Bible College and left with a degree in Theology and a wife, Sue. He then spent 20 years in church leadership, including establishing and leading a Missional Community in the English Lake District, before being called to work with Ellel Ministries. He is a passionate disciple who loves his Lord and His Word and longs for more of God.

When not walking his dog, Poppy, John loves a good film, a good book and setting off on a new adventure!

Printed in Great Britain
by Amazon

21350808R00098